# RESPIRATOR

# DAVID EGGLETON

# RESPIRATOR

## A Poet Laureate Collection

## 2019–2022

OTAGO UNIVERSITY PRESS
*Te Whare Tā o Te Wānanga o Ōtākou*

# CONTENTS

## THREE: PANDEMIC

## FOUR: OLD SCHOOL TIES

## SEVEN: THE WALL

# ONE: CIRCLE

# CIRCLE

Inside whale bone, shark tooth,
inside shark tooth, dog fur,
inside dog fur, albatross wing,
inside albatross wing, kiwi feather,
inside kiwi feather, kākā claw,
inside kākā claw, whale bone.

## TOMORROW

Tomorrow, every now and then, the world might end,
but we will carry on.
Tomorrow, the whistle blows for the start of the week,
and that's where you come in.
Tomorrow is tomorrow, in aroha and sorrow.
Tomorrow is the spice paladin's heated aromas.
Tomorrow is the green flag of hills above window-sills.
Tomorrow is petals, bright and proud on magnolias.
Tomorrow, everything goes in the rumpus room:
the spillage, the abandoned card game,
the unemptied ashtray, the sticky whisky-glass.
Tomorrow is golden chimes, lighting up the lemon tree.
Tomorrow is wild mountain hail, and snow gentle to sea-level.
Tomorrow is tomorrow, in all its iridescence and mesmeric beauty.
Tomorrow, I got your back, and I want to hold your hand.
Tomorrow, we go as inseparable comrades, through the years.
Tomorrow will press you to coal, and then to rough diamond.
Tomorrow, the world is as blue as an orange.
Tomorrow, the world is going micro.
Tomorrow, each of us will follow,
backwards, sweeping the trail clean with a branch.
Tomorrow, see you on the flipside, sistah, in vinyl.
Tomorrow, from drist, rain will dringle and drumble
to form evanescent balms, rinses and vapours.
Tomorrow, more bafflegab, gobbledegook, bumpf,
officialese, taradiddle and blatteration.
Tomorrow, never give in, never give in, never;
in nothing ever give in, except to accede to sense
and deeds of honour, for the sake of others.
Tomorrow, out of black: ka awatea, daybreak,
the ocean immense, eels crossing dark waters;
and above, a mollymawk's glide, tomorrow.

## CATCH

Herding drops of heavy rain,
paddocks settle in paspalum.
Clouds shroud macrocarpa.
The water flexes and wades,
and glides finger by finger,
to join more water, lush
over globed slither of rock,
past gnawed traceries of leaf,
swimming slowly to make
from swampy genesis a river.

## GENERATIONS

Young moths rustle mottoes of dust under
hard rustle of flax, clusters of cracked pods.
An old wētā trawls a sea of forest fronds.
Wasps weave and wrap their pollen trails
over briars loaded with black blood drops
heavier than hearts can bear, for the trees
are our parents' parents, diving down
a millennium underground, bent round
and curled in a birth dream, till the years
unfold roots that twist out of rock fissures,
and climb as seedlings, tender, glowing,
to where bed springs rust in landfill dumps,
in slow tick of rains, and the sulphur creeks
bubble up their finest skim of green scum.

## LUNAR INCANTATIONS

Flower cut in marble,
arum lily's white glow,
curve of a yellow wing,
beam glancing through a window.
A watchful eye reflecting on
spur, spoon, chalice, balloon,
on a delicate coin's worn rim.
Lens in a golden frame,
light made faint when clouds skim,
dreamers' eyes in shadow.

For benefit of flying kites,
the moon will be full tonight.
Coy pose, a bashful glance,
then the moon begins to dance,
launched over a lake of perfect lilac.
In the small hours of the soul,
the unicyclist rides,
slowly across the moon.
And still up there at high noon,
the daylight moon, blue as sky.

## MATARIKI

Matariki's eyes are fiery in the night.
Feather-shawled mountains gleam their beaks.
Great trunks, sawn through, tumble and tilt.
Bold carvings, auctioned in whispers,
echo as prophecies, sung by wind-swept trees.
Plagued by caterpillars, slithered by eels,
a patchwork quilt of farm unravels.
In lightning and hail, each snail snivels;
learned visitors take shelter with skinks,
under rocks from nesting angry falcons.
Ghosts hoard waka in marshes, under silt.
An arcade is roofed with engraved glass;
a pedestal is bound by polished brass;
faces are wound tighter than a watchspring.
Wigs become a sheep flock gathering.
There's daughter of the kauri, Amber Reeves,
sailing for London from the Antipodes.
Through cavern gloom, suspended by ooze,
many worms glow as the matrix broods.

## MOSTLY BLACK

Before, as it was, it was mostly black,
dark beaks, polished talons, feathers, a black
regime drenched in the melancholy black
of rains that took tides further towards black.
From hinges of sunlight hung blocks of black,
and risen humps of islands were matte black.
Cinders sailed from bush burn-offs, carbon black.
Beads on antimacassars gleamed jet black.
Through pine's silent groves possum eyes shone black.
Above tar-seal a melted rainbow turned black.
At disintegration of monolith black,
green, all that blue can be, then back to black.
Green of pounamu lost under lake's black.
Blackout's lickerish taste, blood-pudding black,
and midnight mushrooms gathered from deep black.
Tattoos drawn with bent nib and homemade black.
Batman's mask, a dull sheen of cue ball black.
The primeval redacted, placed in black
trash bags, or else turned out as burnt bone black.
Pull on the wool singlet of shearer's black,
for blacker than black is New Zealand black,
null and void black, ocean black, all black.
In Te Pō's night realm, from Te Kore's black,
under the stars spreads the splendour of black.

## FOUNDATION MYTHS

Having a few,
and then a few more;
elbow working, bottoms
up, down the hatch:
he stews on his own brews,
and steeps them
in conspiracy's deeps.

Hump it or lump it,
stump up or come off it;
full as a bull, bellowing and randy,
looking for a share of hashmagandy.

Holy leftover finger-bones
from an Irish cannibal feast
during the Potato Famine,
brought out as family heirlooms
to add to the cauldron of bubbling gravy.

Seven famines,
seven plagues,
seven crosses,
seven blades —
under seven rains,
green colleens hang heads full of sorrow.
Skimpy, skipped, leafed histories:
harmonics of colonials uneasy in native spaces.

I shuffle chance events
that led me here
on the card table of my mind,

like so many pendants
on a charm bracelet: the padlock,
the heart, the key, the ballet slipper.

The old ones are dying,
and the young ones are struggling to emerge
from a chrysalis of vape fug,
working the room till they find the door
and exit,
exotic to themselves and others,
amid seeds, chaff, straw, a smatter of hail,
out in the fresh air.
The fly's lazy drone
fills the silence,
as the dust-covered box
fills the gap under the roof.

Thickly sprinkled, gritty,
white and grey and black —
ashes of us all,
flung skywards,
make eyes smart, teary.

Ashes in the mouth
taste like vines
burnt at the stake,
in vino veritas:
that charcoal flavour of bottom of bin liner,
bagged and standing out in the rain
at the back of a closed-down restaurant.

## OTAGO EIGHT BELLS

The fetch of the swell
pitched up on the beach
to creak of canvas, splash of oar,
while my rockabilly gait along the shore
is like that of some sailor or Captain Ahab
who rocks a peg-leg made of whale bone.
With quivery wings daylight dances,
embroidered on lacy mist and rosy rain.
White dross drifts and coats
the crosstrees of yachts riding at anchor.
Mist cools summer's festive bouquet.
You might quench your thirst
with a quelled rainshower
grabbed in streaming handfuls
from a hill's wet scarves
of draggled blue delphiniums.
The chill toll of an iron tongue
is calling eight bells
in the mournful wake
of a foghorn out on the harbour,
and something's sailing south,
towards the big swells, said to be higher
than a carpark before
it is pancaked in an earthquake.

## GHOST TOWN

You look a million dollars, old house;
and they say you're worth it,
flossied up with the spit and shine
of brochure talk; you've got it licked,
summery in a dun climate.
The finest music in the world is
korimako calling from a kōwhai tree,
jingle of harness descending the coast road,
belling of a stag like a hunting horn,
the pleasant din of dinner knives,
scrape of lightning-quick forks,
rattle of a hob kettle on the coal range,
church bells, chimes of clocks, horse hoofs,
the rolling of iron-clad carriage wheels,
the shriek of a train whistle.
Moonlight's a ghost town —
silent the grass, silent the sky,
silent the alley, silent the house.

## Sawmill Empire

The history shut up in the book
of a tree opens out in the shape
of a house that sways like a stout
three-master far out at sea.
The arboreal lifts from its foundations.
Between dripping leaves the trees
become hundreds of stairwells
and eaves that lead up to the stars.
Remove an eave when it gets stuck;
it's stripped back to its bare frame,
carved up and trucked off to a lifestyle block.
I am, sang the frame of the house.

Trees were living ancestors
transformed for a bush town,
an enchanted settlement,
while through the cleared canopy
glided the sky, all the way
to the corrugated-iron steeple.
A tracery of wrought-iron sprouted
vines and grapes, mazes and spirals;
friezes filled with quatrefoils, rows of teardrops.
Forest gone to villa, to second-hand
store, to student flat, to antique
shop, to millionaires' row.
From moon-white night, an axe cuts shadow.

Deep-verandahed summer was a sounding-box
of rocking chair, cradle creak, piano notes.
Fretworked and embellished corridors led
to tree stumps and level ground; a door knob

turned for a tea-tray and a spoon's rattle.
Floorboards pressed their tongue and groove;
joists creaked their backs, bending slightly.
Rivers washed up brownish,
sluiced with bark tannins and clays,
or were a silvery arm-wrestle through bracelets
of gravel below the arches of branches,
fluted balustrades, cast-iron sunrises.

Treehouses are barged out of swamp,
and a pole house rises through tree tops
like a moa bird getting above itself;
but some crave eminences to rise from,
so crank dwellings up, and bring them
to headlands, and lower them there,
frail box-kites balanced precariously.
Left to face demolition are elderly tea-rooms,
timber that once ran straight and true,
now warped planks, clapped out, bored through:
wood rotted to punk and dust.
Go map the place, lift the blindfold;
touch crosscut saw, handsaw, jack plane,
smooth plane, brace and set of bits;
trace lost aromas of resin and sap.

The night waltz of houses on the move,
the dancing skeletons of a weekend retreat:
houses shifted on the backs of trucks
to create a new town further round the mountain.
Boards span the air; a drive of logs
funnels along a flume;
the weatherboard city,
lifted from its blocks and piles,

travelling in the wee hours of the morning,
is tunnelling through dreams
into the back country,
where reception committees of iwi
await with taiaha and haka.

## CHRIST THE JUGGLER

Christchurch trembled like a guilty thing surprised,
and, as walls of Jericho to the trumpet blast,
sent up a cloud of archaeological dust,
while high instincts looked to the unperturbed Alps,
shining in their armour of snow and ice,
which looked back like rainbow trout refusing a lure,
at the liquefaction of all that frozen music.
What was once Christchurch, a vast graveyard
of unspeakable secrets locked in Doomsday's vault,
lifted, swayed, shifted, then vanished altogether,
the place of whispering stone went under,
and stairwells to other corridors led nowhere,
no coign of vantage just damp blankets of fog,
swathes of ngaio marsh sunk in miasmic swamp.
Christ, the town launched on flax cordage had snapped.
Fossilised Victoriana broke apart, leaving chunks:
a goody-bag stuffed with lawns, verges, parks,
and new parallelograms of glassy blocks;
keeps where rebuild buildings rose like cruise ships.
Malls are vacuums into which ex-cathedrals rush,
and those soothed by seamless muzak translated from cars.
Fallen the chancel with its old rugged cross;
the crooked house pierced by broken stained glass.
Christchurch, the name, sails on, with Christ's lurch;
basilica smashed like a soft-boiled egg.
Christ the Juggler dropped bricks, opened trapdoors,
and footnoted the labyrinth by walking it, homeless,
with dry horrors, the shakes, delirium tremens,
the ground leaping from dark sleep as if to hug
those who walk on its surface and drag them under.
A fault grinds its teeth in long reaches of the night,

and kids wake from subterranean dreams,
tiny tots of mum's ruin fleeing cracked foundations,
to see beneath a wizard's hat endless road cones,
and Christchurch, crackled grimed colossus, sundered
into a fine-latticed, grisaille city of loss.

## WALNUTS

A leaf storm in autumn.
Walnuts are back down
to earth; they roll
when the hours darken.
A hundred thousand stars tonight
blaze where meteors fall,
to promise a frosty morning.
We bind in measure of a nutshell
the universe,
and extricate the kernel,
encased in quietness.
So seek them beneath the tree.
No more than a walnut in its season,
the brain wrinkles out of reason,
crumbles with a worm inside,
and returns to common clay its pride.

## THE MACKENZIE BASIN

Mountains are sawn, flensed, flogged bone.
Wind blares like trumpets over stone thrones.
By the hay swaddled in bands of green plastic,
skinks bask in tumbled stone under a hunting hawk.
Shelter drawings of kite women climb the burnt
mana spiral to limestone tusks and femurs,
to sculpted claws of reptiles, skulls of eagles.
Silver flashes of young buck salmon pulse
then leap from shadows where the pond thrashes.
Red hawthorn beads sway through cobwebby mists
towards shingle braids that twist down the valley.
A storm seizes the valley by the scruff and shakes.
Mud's transcript is a palimpsest of tractor tyre marks
that weal and groove across farmstay hectares.
Fingers squeak on a fretboard, plink, plank, plunk;
hail on the roof sounds like fence-wire sprung loose;
there are showers of clattering sequins, ice splinters,
and land's white brocade seen through hot tub steam.

## THE WHITE BUTTERFLY

The white butterfly softer than a rose petal
on the sloping lawn flutters down to settle,
and for a moment hangs on a daisy flower
like a half-folded scrap of paper,
then begins furiously flapping fragile wings —
into blue sky it darts and flings,
ecstatic with delight in ragged flight.

Celebrating all the zing in its being,
it zigzags, zigzags up and away,
each wing patterned with smudges of grey,
to dance the dapple of leaf and shadow,
above the garden where cabbages grow.

It slips and dips like a tiny bow-tie
escaped from a shirt collar, that white butterfly,
to join in a closer and closer flurry of white,
like summery snowflakes all through the air,
frantic wings beating a wave of farewell,
as swarms of butterflies float over the trees,
and into the fog of autumn disappear.

# A WEEK IN THE VALLEY

Monday's neighbourhood sticky-beaks
are looking through your window,
wondering where their breakfast is,
tūī wax-eyes bellbirds, the feeder is empty.

Tuesday's kererū glug and gaze, serene,
into their own windows of green.

Wednesday's sash windows rattle up
to their counterweights, and mackerel
shoals hang poised in evening's sky.

Thursday's night moths launch
a jitterbug fiasco against lit windows.

Friday's heavy-breathing possum climbs
a power pole outside the open window.

Saturday's window is embrangled
with tree shadows, and ensorcelled
by owl wings beating quick across the moon.

Sunday is dark and moody, lashing
a grille of rain to every window.

# FRIDGE MAGNET POEM

morning to night

shiver on

happy small refrigerator

off your face

summer through winter

dawn to owl light

whisper this song

I freeze the harvest

from the garden

always so cold

and I make breath cloud

## THE ARCHAIC ORDER

Inside a fubsy dream,
bees treasure summer,
its gorse and bloom entanglement,
its gravid hush before the storm,
in lilac and violet flexure of irises.

Daylight is burnished by bird wings,
by lazy ripples of wind,
as crickets hop about, spiders abseil,
flies waft to hie themselves hither and yon,
a hedgehog rambles, tabby cats yawn.

A sunshower drums light fantastic,
with pitch contour shifting upwards,
fainter and fainter, away,
leaving state house roofs drenched with finery,
so the hydrangea-headed suburb shines.

# The Steepest Street in the World

This, the city so compact it might have been carried
here in a suitcase with wheels, along a road that leads
from the airport with a twirl, headed towards the steep,
very steep, steeper, steepest street in the world.

Where the sky rains potatoes, and rhubarb stalks
grow thick as tree trunks,
and all the pixie houses are sprinkled with stardust,
as the suburbs unfurl towards the steep,
very steep, steeper, steepest street on the world.

Yes, you travel by way of High Street, Angle Street,
Slope Street, Steep Street, Very Steep Street,
Steeper Street, and then you come to it —
Baldwin Street, the Steepest Street in the World.

Where highland pipe bands might caterwaul and skirl
to get their bagpipes and drum majors up it;
and you might go for a burl on a Mini Moke
and barely make it up it: the steep,
very steep, steeper, steepest street in the world.

Whatever happened to those rainy vistas
that used to cover the town for years at a time,
and were so very prominent from the top of the steep,
very steep, steeper, steepest street in the world?

To a Saturday-night frenzy of pre-loaded students
there's only the cliff-top fall, from the steep,
very steep, steeper, steepest street in the world.

Among the things to do in Dunedin when you're dead,
get your hearse to reverse, up the steep,
very steep, steeper, steepest street in the world.

Someone's needed to lead the cavalry charge,
with the roar of a wounded bull, up the steep,
very steep, steeper, steepest street in the world.

If it's no go with Baldwin Street, all we want is a selfie
with a yellow-eyed penguin and a drone's-eye view
from the high road to Larnach Castle, towards the steep,
very steep, steeper, steepest street in the world.

Twenty thousand Aucklanders once flown to the South
by Cadbury's each winter to take part in the Jafa
Rolling Carnival, down gutters of the steep,
very steep, steeper, steepest street in the world.

Bright, orange, citrus-flavoured, chocolate-centred,
hailstorm of lollies playing hardball,
each one Just Another Flipping Aucklander,
rolling down the gradient of the steep,
very steep, steeper, steepest street in the world.

So, hail and farewell Baldwin Street,
for *The Guinness Book of Records*
has taken away your title, to bestow
on a little Welsh lane, of the steep,
very steep, steeper, steepest street in the world.

*But wait! All of a sudden, they've given it back,*
*because their measurements were out of whack,*
*and so, Baldwin, once more you are the steep,*
*very steep, steeper, steepest street in the world!*

## Closed Road

Bushrangers in bowyangs held out billies,
thumped bottlecaps nailed to a stick,
blew foghorn notes across a stone jar's mouth.
The ground trembled, ruptured and stank.

Swaggers had a clay pipe, a sugarbag,
and a kerosene tin of muttonfat to keep
them warm in their road-side bivouac.
Every so often, a rattletrap went past.

Stuck between the dark and the light,
barflies stared into their dust-charged beer,
when they still drank it by the flagon;
then it was hosed away down the gurgler.

Reverends discussed the price of milk,
over china cups of black gumboot tea;
puckered lips, lemon face, announced distaste.
The crux of the matter was volcanic steam.

As milk swayed up to boil in white froth,
a cow-cockie swung from a chandelier like von Tempsky,
big silver spoon between his teeth;
and from a hang of a meringue, mopped up whipped cream.

Anzac biscuits baked in the Calvinist oven,
bee drone each morning, moth hum at evening;
until one nightfall an era ended:
belief buried under a sudden eruption.

# TWO: RĀHUI

# Rāhui: Lockdown Journal

**1.**

Australia's heat map in January
glowed every which way, red, purple, black,
and our skies were made yellow by trans-Tasman smoke,
while scarcely less fraught were dog days of February,
as arrivals drifted through airport duty-free,
in a haze of competing perfume spritzes,
and reports came of a strange virus out of Wuhan,
pale horse and pale rider.

Always to islanders danger comes over the sea;
heat sensors found fever in arrivals from Iran and Italy;
then there was talk of superspreaders,
of clusters in Bluff and on cruise ships,
that made us all nervous.
Some spoke of the sins of the borderless
world being visited upon our people.

Corona once meant halo, but now universal contagion:
viral status only rubbed out by strict sanitisation.
This changes everything, virologists claimed.
The Ides of March announced our new New Year,
when Pasifika was cancelled and things became clear.
Mad psychic weather with moonboots on was closing in,
though it was an Indian summer and days were fine.

**2.**

As Anubis weighs the heart of the deceased
against truth's feather and counts the cost,
in the Egyptian *Book of the Dead*,
so the New Zealand government looked ahead,
and blinked, then said, this is a time of crisis,
and an end to all speculation: full alert, Code Red.

Jacinda arose with the down-home hippy vibe
of a primmer's teacher, newly promoted to principal,
guiding toddlers on a bush walk during a storm,
which has suddenly grown very dark and bleak
from what it was at the start of the week.
Jacinda Influencer, knocking the lid off
and getting to work with the Can-Do mentality,
puts out an order for an imminent lockdown;
her forehead furrows, all must prepare to go to burrows,
or to warrens of burrows, and isolate.
Press Gallery questions coil and whip at sore points,
each answer a lightning rod for more questions.
We are all caught somewhere between a fever dream
and a model predicting rapid escalation.

My ballpoint slides over this journal's white paper
the way a wave's crest is crossed by a surfer,
to leave a foam of excitable scribbles.
Hers is a prohibition, a proclamation, a rāhui —
go hard, or go home: so long, farewell, haere rā.
With a sense of imminent apocalypse and angst,
Kiwis are given just two days' warning
of intent for all to move to live as shut-ins.

**3.**

Sovereign nations briskly airlift out their citizens;
Aotearoa seals itself within the salt-lick
of Te Moana-nui-a-Kiwa, as if, like a cove
bent on skullduggery,
Covid-19 could come ashore at a cove,
under cover of darkness, bearing seeds of strife.
Grasped reins of seahorses, clouds raising anchor:
everybody's clearing off, you bet your life.

The Response rigmarole is trusted: we must prepare,
and anyway it has all bought time,
to have the whole country swing on a dime
and shelter as one, within local habitations.
This is a dog-whistle sheep-round-up issue:
herd the mob together and get them to trot.

Forty-eight hours, town's already looking bare,
as a single seagull sculls up George Street,
slowly its wingtips rise and dip;
soon all towns will be silent and queer
as a five-cornered square with emptiness.
The cancel culture is everywhere.
Abyssinia: in a while, crocodile: after lockdown.

**4.**

Visitors grab their things and run,
the abrupt surge inwards has begun,
leaving the outdoors to the outdoors,
to roving magpie, ravening possum, furtive wallaby,
the antic rantipole stoat that darts bushwards,
the swamp harrier that airily rides a skyhook down.

Oh to sail like a falcon over Franz Josef,
its bluey-white ice, to the grizzled silver
of braided rivers in their mournfulness,
coasting leeward of the Alps, one more time.
Those braided tresses rise out of the skull
of Hine-nui-te-Pō, mountain-white in the night,
and quiver, for she humps earthquake weather on her back,
and each silver braid flexes its own track.

As we close New Zealand's showroom curtains,
it seems an advantage to be distant islands,
even though it's only a small world after all.
A shiny vacancy of rental cars surrounds Queenstown,
and ghostly tumbleweeds bowl along her streets;
no café now does cinnamon toast to go,
and no snowflakes swirl out over the lake.

**5.**

Alert Level 4's all padlock snick, shove of rusty bolts,
lawns being mowed, home repairs being done.
Fear is a plume of airborne droplets;
you may try not to inhale, but that's bound to fail;
best not to go anywhere, just stay here.
Home-alones zone out with headphones.
Travel agents decommissioned; tourist hordes demobilised:
big oil off-shore sucks it up through a straw.

Autumn in lockdown's something half criminal,
half heroic, because, by breaking the rules,
you could get someone infected, even kill them,
so the country expects all to do their duty,
while fallen leaves turn a russet brown,
and rosella parrots flit between branches.

There are briefings daily at 1pm on the TV,
where, calm and collected, Doctor Bloomfield nixes
the bravado of masks, unless you're hospital staff.
Stilts and oystercatchers patrol our beaches,
checking up on invertebrates beneath the sand.

**6.**

Compass needle feels dead set; might get more deadly yet;
couldn't get much higher than Level 4;
how sombrely introspective each face looks.
From front windows, teddy bears, more and more,
stare at the dormant glooms of suburban streets.
All the shopping malls have gone quite quiet,
just rumbling of trucks sidling into docks,
bringing container-loads of perishables:
hot cross buns, well as fruit and vegetables.
April Fool's Day, Bauer Media folds our best bets:
*North & South, Woman's Weekly, Listener* magazine;
though journos storm on Twitter, Bauer has no regrets.

Evening skies from the back porch, half way to nowhere,
go from yolk-yellow to bark-ochre to starry dark.
Sometimes there are borrowings from Tiepolo:
clouds like pink cherubs on a palace ceiling in Venice.
Other nights, the raging orange of Jeffrey Harris,
capturing some high operatic drama;
or else the chill diluted blue of Joanna Paul.
Each dawn brings its own eureka,
and panning the bright fine gold of autumn days.

Experts predict a graph rising like Kaikōura,
towards mountains of the whited dead;
and every frowning emoji on a computer,
stalks the double-fault of eldritch metaphor.
It's closing time in the gardens of the West;
lamplights are burning out all over Europe;
and the virus is a riddle wrapped
in a mystery inside of an enigma,
but we are assured that its code can be cracked.

7.

On social media, shrill trolls moan and mutter
their throw-shade conspiracy schmutter,
but if all the conspirators' theories
were laid end to end to the moon,
I think you're gonna find
they still couldn't bend a single spoon
with their hive mind;
and only Jeff Bezos can levitate
Bill Gates to the pangolin eldorado
at the end of any Amazon rainbow;
while Jacinda Stardust twinkles benignly,
like snow on cloudpiercer Aoraki.

Jacinda Alert, she triggers the alarm,
hammers the message, and nails it home
with the force of a judge's gavel,
to orchestrate the polyphony of 'God Defend New Zealand'
for a godless age; and globally there are requiems
and outlooks grim, while numbers of the dying
go on climbing; and Neil Gaiman
chats about loving the slow pace of life here,
and how he'd like to stay and stay,
then immediately breaks bounds and flies away.

As Covid-19 shuffles closer, like a phantom plague of skinks,
we sink into the domestic like mudfish in dried-up wetlands.
So we might read tomorrow in the tea leaves,
in the smoky taste of lapsang souchong,
or in the gumboot taste of Choysa,
through days of warmish mild weather,
while leaves wind-beaten to bruise-yellow
drop simpering out of the trees.

8.

Māui's fishhook glitters in the sky at dusk,
and earthshine lights up the lunar disc.
In midnight's silence, ghost-calling owls mope,
and mercy errands are dashed on by health workers.
Daylight, from dewy grass, brings forth field mushrooms,
and the pale brown caps of Blue Meanie shrooms.
In Wānaka, they are hurrahing in the harvest;
this year it's a bumper vintage crop.
The grape-pickers are unemployed guides and climbers;
above the must hovers a kind of delicate dust,
that settles its motes through the vineyard air;
while chilly gusts flap the golden tapestry of leaves,
as if to chase out some deeply hidden dragon there.

Here in Dunedin, from within the cocoon we call home,
we contemplate the burl of a Barry Brickell pot,
in which garden flowers unfurl,
and ponder the coronavirus froth
that gargles in compromised lungs
like a mustard gas attack at the Battle of Verdun.
They are pulling the plug out on old-timers
where healthcare's overwhelmed,
as we learn when we nurse to our bosoms
the glimmers of data streams,
held mesmerised and hushed by our screens.

Hedgehogs do battle on the back lawn
like mighty mammoths,
lit up by a torch in the small hours;
and by day there's the humdrum business
of dishwater down plugholes,

and the smell of bread and biscuits being baked.
And everyone plays detective or enforcer,
even dobbing in the wayward Minister of Health,
after photographing his whereabouts by stealth.
The TV has turned into a kind of tureen
ladling out Brown Windsor soup into the bowls
of the masses in the Sabbath calm of every evening.


**9.**


To venture forth for fresh air, like a witness,
is to see each person englobed in amber, on their own island,
or else in lockstep with a significant other,
or with well-exercised dogs;
and then closer, half turned away, apprehensive,
to make a wide berth, give you the swerve like a fata morgana;
and blackbirds, those grave-footed mincers,
haunt wastelands brambled with neglect,
while sentinel thorns surround ramparts of rock,
below a shuttered and barred church,
yellow-striped Level 4 notice pasted to the locked door.

Easter, and children place Easter Bunny cards
in bedroom windows, while cats doze
and vigils are kept by toy figurines
lying abandoned in front yards
where finches flitter,
as some of the young and restless chafe at quarantine
and barge in groups through desolate carparks,
as out of the blue air spins a kererū feather,
and day after day is sunny.

E-bikes whizz by, saddlebags loaded,
the cyclists wearing sunnies and gloved and masked
in splendid isolation.
Iso-bubble drivers are edgy in rear-view mirrors,
in solitary confinement for the duration of their trip,
supermarket-bound before quickly back to lockdown;
and George Street is becalmed at eventide in a brownout,
as if powered down near zero on the grid,
but traffic lights still blink and police cars glide.


**10.**


Moon is underwater, drought is in the land,
Covid-19, curious term, now one we all understand.
No country's neutral, all in thrall to the catchy virus,
and the spectre of economic anarchy haunts
both populist and globalist narratives,
from Britain to Brazil, by way of Washington,
Orbán Bolsonaro to Boris Putin,
Duterte Modi to Marine Trump.

The Anzac Day fanfare is subdued this year
to standing unified apart,
at the front gate, in faint echo of a brass bugle,
as red fills the sky and sunrise flashes on
the instant bronze age of house window panes.
Bright berries glow like drops of drawn blood,
and is that the 'Last Post' catching on the wind,
or just the wheezy hinge of the unlatched gate?
Or is it the cry of the Covid-19 barbarian at the gate,
trying in its pesky microbe way to aggregate?

Some couch-surf all day in an anti-viral fug,
others putter round, play Candy Crush, or want a hug.
I hear Ashley Bloomfield, voice of pragmatic calm,
suddenly say, with a Dalek's krark krark:
Eliminate! Eradicate! Exterminate!
For that is what the Covids hate!
And then his voice pitch-shifts back to normal,
on RNZ National, the sensible public official,
giving his Daily Briefing on the need for vigilance.


**11.**


At last we're descending to Level 3,
a quota of freedom for you and for me,
and it's very nearly May, up in the hills,
we in our sunshot bubble admiring red admirals.
They nest on nettles then dance arrestingly away,
as noon burnishes the long-stemmed ragwort,
pestiferous grand-daddy to all the young ragwort;
and bracken winds spiderwebs down to the clay,
here by the shine of the wind-punished tussock;
and hark, hark, to the lark that trills,
above roofs, stadium, and factory mills.
Weatherwise, the clouds turn dressing-gown grey,
as we get in our car and drive carefully away
from others, following distancing that must be obeyed,
or render perilous the whole blockade.

From Michigan in the USA,
we learn of protestors who boast that they
are willing to take a bullet for their neoliberal beliefs
in the right of consumer choice and the right to Live Free or Die,

and that to follow rules of social distancing
is to be brainwashed in a Communist laundry,
with your mind pleated and steam-ironed to uniformity:
net result, virus spread increases and more people die,
the uncanny like wildfire leaping from host to host.
As PM Ardern said, it's a pandemic, damn it —
and you assemble at your peril and your loss.

Trump, at first, advised Americans just to relax,
and carry on with eating to the max;
and then he changed this soothing tune,
for a sinister dirge of blame and blame again,
anyone he thinks is lame, or in his way.
Although a proven liar,
he promises a miracle cure,
and drinks his pepped-up quinine
with a horrible equine whinny,
making tasty smacking noises through tiny lips.
Never say never, but Americans ever
need to trace the rona with a scanner,
then hit it with lockdown's hammer till it's done,
or the menace will go on menacing forever and a day,
and America's very fabric continue to fray,
in a kind of Fantasy Sci-Fi Horror Thriller show.

**12.**

Now the month of May advances,
the skies are bright and clear,
Orion's belt turns, the Southern Cross blazes,
in this Plague Year.
A black river careers deeply through the gorge,
as the last embers of sunset are snuffed out;
so it's bravo to frontline nurses both here
and overseas, while our teams largely prepare
to stand down, as we get ready
to go down to Level 2 on 14 May,
when you can get a takeaway from a café
to take home;
and while at first no more than ten
at a pinch can be together,
if the logging of new cases stays steady at nil,
then in a week or maybe a fortnight,
a hundred souls can gather
as their birthright,
without fear of the long tail.

Finance Minister Grant Robertson,
who has dispensed largesse of money
for the sake of the economy,
on Budget Day promises further subsidy.
Hopes are that, thanks to track and contact trace,
the least person will not be found out of place,
before the next wave breaks
on a further shore for a more weary nation.

So the future's not what it used to be, nor are we,
and here we go, here we go, here we go,
or rather here we stay;
and is that Teddy on the window sill still,
and will we go back to Level 3,
and will there be jobs for you and me, after lockdown?
This is the end of autumn, the end of May,
and we are backing into a southerly,
towards the warmest winter ever,
while in the garden in the sunshine,
a heavy kererū clings,
like a happy homing pigeon
to the branches of a favourite tree;
and by the sugar nectar feeder a bellbird sings
and a bumblebee bumbles
and the tūī argue at high frequency.
Ominously,
I read online in *USA Today* that American
columns of the sick and columns of the dead
march in ever greater numbers.
As humans, we are always approaching and leaving normal.
Deep breaths then, and a slow and even breathing.
Breath is a vapour. Skin is a porous border.
A poem is a kind of respirator.

*Ōtepoti Dunedin, March–May 2020*

# THREE:
# PANDEMIC

## TEAM SPIRIT

Cook Strait scopes out coast on both sides.
A possum tail quivers like a fern-tip dancing.
Moa bones are assembled as the chosen ones.
Two teams, north and south, are advancing.

Eyes flicker open on wintry weather,
like bright nails hammered in old sheet iron.
We raise our phones till they vibrate together;
we'll save victory celebrations to put online.

He's done decent time; he was once dog tucker;
but he came back still breathing; she was beaut
in an oilskin parka, keeping it together;
we knew game on, after they got there in the ute.

Rains ravish ravines and fields are full of water.
Rucked-down, the back row rips free, then races.
Spectators hoot, like when they release owls
to rouse bats that roost in the wrong places.

A good clean ball has been fed to the scrum,
but they respond with oodles more niggle.
Lugged from Luggate to the Land of Mordor,
pulled from the maul, he scores with a jiggle.

That bloody go-getter's upping the ante,
squinnies at the wind, takes three steps backwards;
nothing too fancy, pots pill between posts.
Rugby boots sink in turf, soft and spongy.

Ball's lobbed to the line-out, like an apple
with a grub inside thrown at the mongrel
tearing at a dead sheep to say, Get lost.
The time to get a kick away is ample.

A maggoty young player springs for the skies,
with the legendary leap of a flea.
The ball moves fast as something greased;
a butterfly slides sideways in the breeze.

The gun winger receives ball, takes his punt,
follows up, a pig-dog chasing a boar.
Grabs it, gets thumped, and ball turns headless chook,
under the wonky arm of a legless thinker.

As a shoulder charge in a crowded booze barn
knocks wool from heads, puts the score on the line,
he's gone shaky as a lean-to in a southerly;
offers fifteen ways of saying, Really?

Each team turns antic, each one's hanging on,
till a try gets converted in extra time,
under doleful eyes of the losing side —
mate, who'd want to be on the losing side?

# PANDEMIC

Pandemonium. Pandemonium.
Order disaster with a wheelie bin,
lift the lid, pour out all within.
Taste wildfires, inhale smoke,
hunker on Zoom, try to look woke.
Crystals, hung as mobiles, go splenetic.
Go nowhere in this pandemic;
shelter in place. Masks as hot
as hot breath on each face.
Hands put together, pushed apart.
Vulcan greetings, given from the heart.

Pandemonium. Pandemonium.
Lonely islands loom, stock-still,
like container ships under sun's grille.
The world pre-Covid has gone under;
scent of hand sanitiser hangs in air.
Nīkau palms stretch to the sunset.
Well met, but keep your distance from me.
Fever hides from border detection,
in all these knots of connection.
Some sicken, some die, some get well soon.
Our looking glass is the far-off moon.

Pandemonium. Pandemonium.
Each month advances, margin by margin.
Mortality rides a winged gas-guzzler,
over the perimeter, over the border.
Brandish the brand; a bright sword
throws lances of light to bring us word.
Full moon tonight, a blood moon,

then a supermoon, full of blood.
Not for gardens is the earth turned aside,
lament each life lost, numbers mummified
by the News into one mighty sarcophagus.

Pandemonium. Pandemonium.
A terracotta army transported, we gaze up,
into the night sky, beyond the telescope.
Anguish might crack and fry each screen.
Riders storm the night, apocalyptic in dream.
Out there, Covid-19, with grim pomp
and ceremony, traces its destiny.
We stay home, we stay quiet in our lanes,
lit by reflections of approaching flames.
Though clouds of uncertainty flocculate,
we know that a needle can inoculate.

## AUTUMN ALMANAC

March begins and this isn't Flint, Michigan,
this is Waikouaiti, so why the toxic tap flow,
chemical warfare creeping through a waterhole?
Self-harmer farmers in a town called Malice,
and all the screens hand-held to make you jealous.
Way out here on the borders of disorder,
things that you look at get smaller and smaller.
The price of a house measured in skyrockets,
pieces of string and very deep pockets.
Anonymous veto, not for profit's got to go;
marginal is as marginal does at zero times zero.
Pete Dutton takes out the trash for compaction,
with all the compassion of a bog of liquefaction.
In his *Jurassic Park* mind he's top dinosaur,
as psychopathic as Mohammed bin Bone-Saw.
The bonza Enza's sending its marvellous foils
over glammed-up bubbles, but Prada's on stilts,
risen from the wine-dark chops and whipped tops
of meringue waves that plunge Zespri-green,
by containers stacked like pandemic coffins.
Hydrofoils, peppermill and salt grinder:
America's Cup yachts, flying a blinder —
till Luna Rossa sinks like a stolen handbag.
You are the Alpha and the Oprah agog,
check the righteous princess, the Windsor frog;
Lorde knows, we will never be royals on TV,
but at least we got water trucks in Waikouaiti.
Quakes made the ocean dance like Beyoncé's
booty-bounce over from the Kermadecs;
everyone hit the decks like nervous wrecks,
but it all fell flatter than a soufflé,

and Queenstown's a limbo-dancer in limbo,
go low, go lower, get your lawyer on the blower.
The bang-on-a-can brigade leave the smelter,
carrying all the aluminium they will ever need
for tinfoil hats and the dross of anti-5G.
Destiny and Tamaki are revving up a Harley,
oozing oily unction, greasy hair and skin.
What he quotes is not quite from the Bible,
and what he preaches is almost libel.
So many contradictory narratives —
anti-vaxxers swear each is an eye-witness.
They don't believe in an interventionist jab,
or in Jacinda Ardern's gift of the gab,
but have faith in swarms of micro-aggressions
by Mike Hosking in his minute-long sessions —
more outlandish, the better they like them.
There's Cruella Collins and her 101 Damnations:
devilish thoughts of Covid-weakened nations
climbing to the top of decline and fall;
you will know them by their trail of the dead.
Autism, colonialism, evangelism, behaviourism
are shades of the doxology economy.
Feel the hot breeze of aggressive reason,
anarchist or rationalist for the Hollywood LOLs
of Bezos Zuckerberg and the Deadly Hallows.
Locked out, locked in, locked up, locked down:
when can everyone go mask-free, town to town?
When can the cray-cray king get a new crown?
There's the horoscope, the personality quiz,
the credit rating and the clickbaiting.
I got a gut feeling, everyone's waiting.

*Ōtepoti, 16 March 2021*

# IMMUNITY

Immunity is a juice, sugar-free.
Immunity, environ me.
I see immunity, the far-off land,
where grey power turns to grey powder,
sprinkled on the sea.
Twitter feeds a line of bird seed
straight into a box you make
with your hands to signal
you're on someone's camera
as a prismatic screen persona,
curated, purified, absent no longer
than it takes to say, What's the data say
about collective murmuration?
Anonymity is a form of immunity
for only so long.
The trains are seething across the suburbs
like zip-tags, doing and undoing postal codes.
The trains are empty carriages,
though sometimes dotted with citizens
using their phones to calculate risk,
to calculate immunity.

## ODE TO THE CYCLEWAY

Too much smashed glass on asphalt,
swerving in and out of the bike lane,
you got skaters, scooters, vapers,
someone taking selfies with boozers.
Everyone is insane after dark,
by the locked park gates;
and where do you park so no one
can pancake the car roof off a balcony?
Someone's playing housie with a trust fund,
someone's put the rent up on white fragility,
someone's hurled cookie dough on the pavement.
Fang it, prang it, walk away totalled,
who's got the price tag of that?
Shuffle to the muffler, raise the wheels,
or tow it away from the harbour,
after raising it out of the water.
Seepage, salvage, knock-down heritage;
raise up flower power in gardens.
Let the chips fall where they may,
on airwaves, sheathed in hagfish glue,
or stuck to the highway back
when yesterday was some place to be.
Asphalt shades of greyscale
unscroll a doomslayer's papyrus,
its dried-up syrups of blood, lead, nitrate.
Gaps are bridged by sighs, years by stars
that might scratch your eyes out.
The fevered rain is not enough to wreathe a sinkhole.
Cram cranberries in your gob by the handful,
and click through dross after dross on ways
to improve the biosphere from inside your silo.

The checkout counter, like your personal biomass,
counts somewhere, maybe.
And you were born and raised in a coffin,
and now you're an astronaut on a mission,
your ashes are launched from a circus cannon,
towards a trampoline you pre-ordered,
from your parked-up car above Lover's Leap.
Peeps are posting pics of themselves planking,
or leaning away from the goalposts,
looking down on a mass grave called Planet Earth.
Ashes drilled into the skin with a needle are blue.

## ANZAC DAY THUNDER

Fields of red flood Sunday's sky
over Queens Gardens Dawn Parade,
and people's thoughts turn to Gallipoli,
carved by trenches, where history
fought history, and Otago's
H.D. Skinner took a potshot
at Kemal Ataturk on horseback,
but only creased his hair or hat,
or some such legend or lie,
in the War to End All Wars.
And now autumn continues dry
and warm, and tree leaves glow red
above wide-spread fluorescent road cones.
We ride our bikes to Port Chalmers,
for a boat trip across the harbour.
A drooping flag snaps to attention
at sound of thunder, a storm mention,
as Rachel, the skipper of MV
*Sootychaser*, grabs hold of each bike
to lift them onto a rack; then past
Quarantine Island we motor,
butting the swell, to our Peninsula stop,
while a squall swings by and the sea dashes,
lit up, as if by gun muzzle flashes.
Down the windscreen of the vessel
raindrops squirm, like an ogre's drool.
Through razzle-dazzle, we progress.
In the distance, yachts buck and toss.
A rainbow's shawl covers Harbour Cone.
There's ghosts of feathery snowfall
from hail-studded heaven on stone,

as we wallow next to Broad Bay jetty,
drawn up close by the skipper's skill.
Haloed in quarrels of rain-arrows,
past the humpy hill of Portobello,
under fierce weather, bent almost askew,
we cycle through gale's winnow,
all the way to the Taiaroa Heads,
home of the albatross colony
on a bluff hooked like a bird's beak.
There, northern royals veer
to dip or tilt, in windshear,
or swoop and soar like gliders,
while we twisting bike riders seek
to blunt the bite of flying grit.
Soon we pedal back, into a stiff wind,
as every tree and bush ripples.
The road is low along the shoreline,
where in summer a tide of red krill
bloomed like harvests of strewn petals.
Finally, the sky's clear and fine,
but the southerly still funnels
relentlessly above the burrows
of South Dunedin, and greyish waves
wreathe and unwreathe, crests stained
red as poppies by late Anzac Day sun.

*April 2021*

# THREE HAIKU

*Spider*

Parachutist sways
silk canopy;
a sailor, crafty
in rigging.


*Curtained Room*

Potted fern plant
in curtained room,
lives on
the memory
of sunlight.


*Dog Days*

Raindrops give
puddles
goosebumps,
and comb hairs
on a dog's head.

## PROTEST

Jolts and ruckus
lambaste swarms
and hives;
ant trails wave
placards
of fear and anger
at whatever's out
there that doesn't
care but looks on
with the languor
of big cats lifting
a paw — the smears
are human tears.

## THE TONGUE TRUMPET

Is all the money dumb? Uh-huh.
Is everybody asleep at the wheel?
Will you be my spiritual adviser?
What is the fastest way out of here?
Has the globe slowed down, and
does it mean we all have to get off,
because the next stop is Alpha Centauri?
One day, it's like a miracle, it will disappear.
You know what I'm talking about.
Believe me, what a difference a day makes.
And I'm yours, whatever it takes.
Make mine zabaglione, with
a glass of Zsa Zsa Gabor vintage.
Fly me to the moon. Please, please me,
all the way to Tinseltown in the rain,
and those crazy clown cars, every home
should have one. Plug it into the wall socket.
Bada bing, bada boom. I'm here shaking
my ding-a-ling, yelling for the 7th Cavalry.
We've had very few deaths, watch my lips,
and they've been largely old people, who are,
if not expendable, certainly susceptible
to what's happening. These are all very fine people,
by the way. And how do I know so much
about this? Maybe I have a natural ability.
I really get it. It's just who I am, Mr Natural.
How big a game-changer could horse tranquilliser be?
How about its sister drug, the de-wormer?
I'm a big fan. I feel good about it. Just a feeling.
Up, up and away to my beautiful orange buffet.
And then I see the disinfectant,

where it knocks it out in a minute,
because it gets in the lungs and it does
a tremendous number on the lungs.
Have you ever heard of that as a cure?
I have a high approval rating, and when I tested
positive I said to my people, We will get through
this together, because the other people don't matter.
Well, what are you going to do?
A plane goes down, 500 people dead. They don't
talk about that, you notice the news now, right?
All they ever talk about, and here's the thing
— is everybody asleep at the wheel?
But there's never been anything like this.
And I've been around. Believe me.

## KEY TO THE HERMIT KINGDOM

Once far to the back, now far out in front,
to bear the brunt and wear the shame,
the Minister of Health arrives by stealth;
children have assembled for the bull-run.
The basis of life in these islands is sun.
Random offence takes knee-jerk exception
to a nation's internet solipsism.
They want to topple statues, wave through
freedom protestors, tweeters who invite you
to burn replicas of JK Rowling at the stake,
or shout cancel in Putin's graffitied face,
then pose on Insta to game the blame.
As yesterday's video static unspools,
white noise buzzes across the tells
of a whole world in bruise-coloured blue,
globe mortified by heat-wave distortion,
though too we might die of rabid exposure,
our tarpaulins snatched away by storm cells.
Our gathered thoughts await their closure;
while all look on, thanks to their devices;
and beware the naked blade that flashes
in dearer supermarket chainstore aisles;
beware pop pop pop of police gunshots,
attempts to liberate property from capital.
When asked, step away from those unmasked;
accept the chill vaccine that burns the arm.
Everything depends on the arrival
of red wheelbarrows from China for big-box stores,
before the globe's supply chain breaks again:
the ever-remoter quota of Autumn's dry spell
frozen, like jagged truths of rock pools drained,

those barren rocks where marooned sailors listen
for the lure of mermaids and police sirens.
Winter's stew of hot news, of anonymised outrage,
lasted the season in Key's Hermit Kingdom.
Then jet-set Spring arrives, tanned and smiling,
in a jeep over sand, towing Summer's caravan,
which brings an all-weather finish to year's end.

*January 2022*

# A Poem for Waitangi Day

## I

From the Void, Te Kore, seven kinds of light:
first, glowworm glimmer; then silvery gleams;
next, a mauve aura; the stars grow fainter
as Papatūānuku moves apart from Ranginui;
the land is the colour of Governor Grey;
then brighter beams follow; before summer's
brassy Rātana band clarity emerges;
and down in the gully we walk out into the sun,
crossing the creek as if time has just begun.


## II

We wave charms and amulets,
horoscopes and horticultural guides
to best brands to buy
for Generation XY,
Generation Alibi.
All in this waka together,
bombarded by small pieces of pumice and scoria;
so emotionally invested
in Kiwiland's avatar —
where we the people, we the sheeple.
We the peeps, we the perps,
we the fraudsters, we the Treaty-honouring,
dwell and dwell
on a happening turned into an awakening,
as moody evening loses its clandestine lighting.

Can't hongi with poets, just elbow-bump
at a hāngī for the queen;
lower masks, rub noses, and tipple a snifter
of Baileys Irish Cream.
Bring home ashes in a trim hessian bag:
those lately gone to the realm of Hine-nui-te-Pō.
The manes of white-haired New Zealanders
nod sagely like toetoe plumes in the breeze.
The CEO's a paladin who just lost his rag:
a prince of millionaires
with a Herne Bay helipad.
Plenty of bottom end to go around the bend;
a magistrate's gravelly speech,
throws the rule book in a straight line,
as southern rātā and pōhutukawa
paint the whenua red.


## III


Place-names vanish, to be replaced
by what Papatūānuku dreams,
when the motu turns over in its sleep
and rumbles and steams.
Root vegetables bake delish in a dish;
I speak of the potato and the kūmara.
Commended souls do eye-rolls.
The festive season has its reasons.
The dire-wolf bares its teeth
to express grief;
puddles exclaim with pelting rain;
myriad tones of voice let rip
to the muffled hills as one song,

through the car window's quarter-light.
The rubble of jaded intellects is landslip.
If this be Doomsday, it is not in jest.
Isolation with the hard borders of lockdown
declares the importance of being earnest.


## IV


Here come the clouds; how vapid they are,
as if texting each other with sun emojis,
or pursuing futile chases that dissolve
into future expanses of climate change.
The lazy wind gives a farewell wave and dies;
a tsunami rolls and rolls,
far-out as a January day,
foamy as a car-wash.
Beneath the calm surface of bland
quivers a passive-aggressive possessive
that whips out like a lizard's tongue
to drag home its target like a wrapped-up fly.
Silly old fossil fuels flow from Noah's flood;
there's reverence and sublimation in hydro-electric structures.
Will the weather never get green?
It's going to be a fly-by of better loyalty cards
through blue skies from now on,
and a free Sweetwaters concert in every rest home.

There's a convenient convenience store,
but no public convenience to be seen.
There's abject poverty up there on the screen,
but it's quickly covered by a request
to recycle your mosaics of microplastics downstream

for a pre-packaged lunch deal and a bank loan scheme.
Shoegazers on TV denounce single-use.
Low tolerance levels are expected to increase.
Seals flip and glide and swim in-shore.

The sacred nacre of pāua, spit of oyster spat,
a smelt blaze and the tag of string flutter;
starred wire fences cut across contours;
the falling folds of the bush-line
are petticoats of green crinoline.
Musculature of rugged ranges,
coloratura of operatic tūī,
chaffing of chaffinches,
beady wax-eyes that cluster in view,
a rumour of rosellas, a squabble of sparrows.
Flipped vortex of a spinning top;
lawn rolled up like carpet and flung on a truck.

There's pounamu that dwells in a tapu pool
to be prised and appraised anew,
as a stoned head bends and lends an ear,
while marl rebuffs the translucent īnanga.
Brisk claw and scrape of a twig by a kākā;
kererū going for it — the reddish berry,
with bunt and swoosh, sough and shush.


V


A chain-link alphabet strains around the massive
neck of a kauri tree, and talismans are token
in this one hundred percent pure Arcady,
the Lord knows where, throwing shade and azure.

It is, in semblance, a looking-glass land,
a solid gold golf ball whacked into the gulf;
moth-land, moon-land, shear-land, gland-land,
whose North Island might checkmate South Island,
and take as pawns Stewart Island, the Poor
Knights, the Great and Little Barrier
bishops in a game of Crown and Anchor.
And let the glacial attitudes of the Pākehā
melt like snow creatures, or ice crystals,
in the eerie green faery mist
of patupaiarehe, amid chants of atua;
then bring out the chart of Te Tiriti o Waitangi,
document stained with blood and squid-ink.
A flying canoe ghostly in the sky paddles
over the whole fished-up archipelago,
guided by Kupe, whose pointing finger
shines with shark oil as the stars rise.

*February 2022*

## As Heard on RNZ National's *Morning Report*

You know what matters,
what really really matters?
I'll tell you what matters,
what really really matters.
What really matters,
that's what matters,
that's what matters,
what really really matters.
Now I've told you what matters,
it matters,
it matters that I've told you
what really really matters.
I said no then, I'm saying no now,
and I'll say no tomorrow.
No yesterday, no today,
and certainly no more tomorrow.

## FRIENDS

I'm friends on Facebook with some bots,
some computers I don't really know;
your friendly presence seems familiar,
so friendly, but, really, friendless:
friends with benefits befriending friends with deficits.
Not unfriended, but with so many friends
assembled, together, apart —
friends of friends of friends of friends —
friends, let us recall our friendship.
For we are friends after all,
and arguments with friends being
the basis of the attention economy,
where everybody's a bit antsy,
a bit antsy-in-the-pantsy.
Friends, let us bond over Big Brother Zuckerberg,
though he has no more personal interest in us
than in a dead fly being hoovered up
from under his desk by an office cleaner
from the Philippines, sympathetically —
but no low blows — 'cos
hatred makes you ugly and we are friends,
with our knee bends, for which we are
pleased to have knees, and our split ends,
if you have ends to split.
The good times are going under to the voice
of thunder in the global echo chambers,
so prepare yourself, friends, for the end of the party line.
Just kidding friends, bantz and lolz;
though, if you click like you will be right,
'cos friends be like friends who emoji you
into the slipstream with a very smiley beam —
so all good, frenz.

# AUTOGEDDON

Horn cadences bray; storeyed carparks climb. On the Spaghetti Western motorway, thoroughbreds gallop, nags limp, and tall trucks wobble like prairie wagons.

Nearing traffic-cone country, highways clot to snail pace. The hi-viz vest squad in earmuffs weed-whacks a berm. Beeping to get a wriggle on, stuck in crawlspace, a driver chews her bubble gum to boiling point.

Bull-bars bunt like antlers; paddle-pops guard zebra crossings; cat's eyes blink; skateboarders bumper-hang; tyre tread signs the dotted line. The tailback jam's a slow-moving glacier, compounded of frozen glances and tiny fists beating against insides of windscreens.

Past the bottleneck, traffic swarms as one, like wasps from a nest knocked out of a tree. Motorbike throttles open up on the scenic route. Mag wheels revolve quickly over slick tar-seal, but pause delicately for the breath-testing queue.

Out of the dark heart of night cars transform, with flashing grilles and sleeved headlamps and aerodynamic stripes, to samurai warriors, to the judder of kabuki theatre, to racer circuits between stoplights. Truckies ratchet up the ante and gun their big rigs; possums are mashed into pizza topping.

End of the road is Autogeddon's scrapheap: confiscated, crushed, melted for road signs.

# FOUR: OLD
# SCHOOL TIES

# HONE

Poet of the brouhaha, of the feed of oysters;
voice a dry cackle, or plummy, plush,
lickerish, lavish, mellifluous, mellow.
Poet of truth, a smoke, and beauty, mate.
Poet of jugs of amber in the arvo;
whenever you met a broke of poets
propping up the public bar, and you were flush,
you always insisted on your shout.
Poet of cabbages and orange monarchs,
poet of the hue and cry, poet of the Māori people,
poet of the hīkoi, of flax roots; poet for the lonely,
for the peripatetics and the melancholy;
for the easy-oozy and the woozy-doozy,
in a taxi on the way to a party;
for the hair of the dog whipped up with an egg whisk.
Poet of the rhododendron rodomontade; poet of AA.
Poet blundering like a fat moth into the sunshine.
Poet with voice growly as a possum, chewing through
Orsman's *Dictionary*.
Poet skating verbal figure-of-eights delicately,
pen held as taiaha.
Maestro, maître, piano accordion voice resonant
on the Left Bank of the Waikato River;
poet holding up Mayakovsky's megaphone
in the face of the minister;
poet who led the people's army of poets
out of the People's Palace and into the pub.
Poet of the aroha of the hug, poet of the hongi,
poet croaking contentedly in the rain.
Poet who would phone and say, On any
scrap of paper handy, please write down

this poem I wrote today.
Poet who floated out,
spouting like a pilot whale off Kaka Point.

## DEAR READER
### Thoughts after looking at CK Stead's poem 'That Derrida Whom I Derided Died'

'Derrida, enemy of plain sense, my enemy too ... handsome face,
white hair ... intellect loyal to nothing but itself ... Critical parricide ...
a ghost ... a voice ... a word ...'

The great white shark under mackerel skies,
CK Stead has heaved into view:
that CK Stead who sees theory and therapy
as twin spectres haunting Enzed poetry.
Not for Stead the paralysis of analysis,
he gets out and does, he socks it to the man.

Gate-keeper, chucker-out, culture-bouncer,
calls out Derrida as French for horse's posterior.
Stead of the Overflow, with his totemic cranium,
hunting for the snark, hunting for the subtext;
floats like a pūriri moth, stings like a German wasp.
The drive-by, take-down guy, with silver hatchets
and bloody scalps stacked in his trophy cabinet.

Brain like a buzzsaw, cutting away dead wood,
wants his poems to shine out like good deeds,
plain as common sense in a naughty world.
CK Stead, CK Stead, was it something I said?
Are you vexed I said you must deconstruct the text?

When Tennysonian shades tread in sadness
and mourners impute elegiac otherness
to the manliness of Hopkins, and waves
like little Rudyards come Kipling in from Babylon

and Timbuctoo and Nineveh and Pompeii
to the pyroclastic dawn over Rangitoto,
to this hamlet of Parnell where ghost of Hamlet's
father walks his own Elsinore,
then Derrida, that Lazarus, that phoenix, that volcano,
announcing every container ship contains the unreadable,
Derrida who crooks his Baudelairean pinkie,
tied like a thread to the coffin of literature,
as the writing that writes goes on writing,
that Derrida goes on dying, and CK Stead too,
in his Parnell fastness, the last of his crew.

Stead overflows boundaries as the sea threatens to do,
harbouring a buoy or two, and bloated authors
wash up dead to the bark of a dog named Barthes,
paddling his paws in the writing which writes
page after page of white foam on black rocks of home,
while the sea creaks its hinges to seagull whinges.

## SARGESON TOWERS

'The Sargeson offers NZ contemporary design with two
six-level towers … The Sargeson presents the ultimate lifestyle
of convenience in the heart of Takapuna.'
                                    *– real estate advertisement for Sargeson Apartments*

Not in narrow seas light fires of no return,
nor where blows the wind of fruitfulness,
but at dead low tide amongst brooding mangroves,
while the crab scuttles, the lone gull crarks,
and the mudflat poets gather buckets of cockles.
A plumb bob swung through an open portal
might leave us no wiser as to where we are,
but think of it as Auckland in the 1950s,
crossing the pitch and toss of the Waitematā
on a harbour ferry, to the fabled poverties
of the North Shore bohemians trying to survive
in Grog's Own Country when bliss was it to be alive,
under an overstory of mythic timber heights,
lately cut down and burnt to black stumps.
So, a window opens in a villa's kauri heartwood,
and a hooting ruru doubtfully eyes the dawn.
Oh, for the days when every town had a fountain,
jetting coloured water, pinks and greens, like a dream
of what might yet be spouted in Takapuna, where
Keith Sinclair plays tea-chest bass, Smithyman's at the forge,
and in sackcloth and ashes McCahon sips bodgie's blood.
From Bruce Mason's navel, thespians wander and yarn,
stewing on the rhubarb-rhubarb of a play's first night.
Then the smoky green, countersunk, koru spiral,
sly mileage of a coastal steamer, a yacht groping a zephyr,
dense gloom, hidden light, Grafton Cemetery vapours,

volcanic caves glowing with spittle of worms.
A thousand city planning boo-boos owned up to,
that barge Glover sat in, poled by King Rex Fairburn,
shorewards to the tootle and fife of good old Sarge,
leading the way to gleaming jugs of Lemora,
and a sugar-sack full of withering lemons,
beneath a skull-white George Wilder moon.
In the Lounge Bar, ladies perch on the good chairs,
as if pubs might be shrines to higher thoughts;
in the public bar, blokes get soused on bowsers of booze,
swearing that the longest word they know is corrugated-iron.
They howl, miaou, bark and bray; they yell hooray.
Outside, sparrows settle on toetoe plumes to peck away.
Enter the poet with a face like a map of New Zealand,
ARD Fairburn, all his china ducks lined in a row,
announcing free potshots for young and old,
as the beer goes flat and the ashtrays stale.
Here's the New Zealand of how are you getting on,
here's the New Zealand of get out of it yah mongrel,
the New Zealand of get stuffed, get a gorse bush up yah,
get back to from where you came,
get away and never darken our Customs shed again.
Then Rex steps forth like a pūkeko risen from mānuka,
the alchemical man with gladiator sandals,
saying *Don't talk wet* and *Pour us another one.*
He's got an affinity with eels, with damsels and dragonflies,
launches into a riverrun of Finnegan's wakespeak,
claims he's lost his marbles, but most of them are in his mouth.
Like flagpole halyards whistling in the wind, sings Rex
of the blab of the pave, the paper boy's call,
a wolf whistle from the railway station bookstall,
the boys raising crown-and-anchor on a tarry bit of canvas,
Maurice, Maurice and Maurice tapping typewriter keys,

ivory towers making hay bales into learned academese.
Bob Lowry's on the rocks with the Opononi dolphin;
RNZAF Mason makes his books into flying boats,
and skates them off the end of the Devonport Wharf.
Then hail crashes like a flail to clear the muggy air,
for the romantic North Shore's dead and gone,
it's with ARD Fairburn in the graveyard,
and so is the Sarge, and all the Sons of Sarge,
and now only brand-new Sargeson Towers stand
as deluxe living for those with ready cash in hand.

## On First Looking into James K Baxter's *Collected Letters*

World within world within world,
fallen out of a storybook
years ago, yet confined within
my cranium, below which
crooked bones creak and limp,
awkward as could be,
religiously cycling, tilted
electric Limes glide along the line,
turning roads that skein
to tangle round the town's
traffic jam, going home for tea.

Carefree, I'm no more chastised
by the hangman's beautiful daughter
who lived in a gypsy house-bus
that toured from fair to fair,
and who became vampiric,
a warted soak weaving her way
to the anaesthetist's cabinet,
her ear cocked for the intricate makers,
at their ticking altar of dictionaries,
at their stage-crafted priestly business,
Aleister Crowley, Rosaleen Norton,
two parts glory, three parts damnation.

That was a time when
in Faustian splendour we dawdled
out the daylight moonshine,
waiting for the coffins to open
and begin their after-dark service,
fiddling at the door to the vault.

Under the weight of those days,
bent nearly double, ghosts stumble on,
the Remmers bank managers,
bald as the pavement they tripped along,
the untouchable Epsom girls
who strode reciting grammar,
the stern matrons who chaperoned weakly,
the boneshaker postal truck that puttered,
me with my skeleton key limbs
who disported ironically,
spun seaward, landward, windward,
who finally tottered to heart's ease,
and ancient whispered hymns,
all that never was and never again.

The cloud appreciation society
in a state of bliss at cumulus,
poured like foamed milk from a pitcher,
arthritic boomers bent round in koru spirals.

Those who rattled their keys, going ballistic,
garbling their words daily, hypocoristic,
appealing the length of the sentence as un-Kiwi,
all fully present at the wave, wave, wave,
now an emoji, an acid, pot, peyote hashtag.

The psychedelic moment meant
the perfume of feijoas ripening
on the overloaded tree in the abandoned back yard,
whiff of Sunlight soap fragment
on the white basin's seamy craquelure.

Stretch and Ratso went in dead march in October,
bringing up the rear of Hēmi's funeral,
processional, reverential, though themselves 400
kilometres north of Wanganui
in Auckland at the time, asleep,
dead drunk at the kitchen table
of a crash pad that crashed long ago.

## SOUNDS OF THE SIXTIES

They're changing guard at Buckingham Palace;
a Wolf Cub calls: Kennedy's dead in Dallas.
Rhubarb's growing; Dad's nailing wire-netting;
Mum's over the fence, having a natter.
I'm listening to Aunt Daisy, to horse race betting.
The atomic bomb is what's the matter;
it's on the air, it's the dust of my despair.
My mother's baking; I hand her the vanilla essence.
In the back yard's 44-gallon drum, newspapers flare.
I watch heat haze waver above the rim of rust;
missing pages wrap round a .303 bolt.
Once, time was a shoulder of lamb with mint sauce;
hydrangeas flowered to a clear sky blaze.
The cat scampered lawn to chase butterflies.
I dived towards a Kodachrome-blue pool, untold.
Night held fire sirens; Dad had a wristwatch of rolled gold.
Radio valves crackled; air smelled of burning.
The doors of the bank revolved; years went on turning.

Chalk snapped and dusters clapped in the classroom.
Peter Snell flashed a broad grin when he pounded
around the track, as we small kids gabbled
and, excited, sought his autograph, scrawled in silence.
Friday's newspaper parcels we grubbed fingers on,
to pluck from torn steamy vents soggy chips.
Saturday arvo, Jaffas bowled down floorboards at the flicks.
On Sundays, hair combed back with Brylcreem,
the ballad of 'The Man Who Shot Liberty Valance'
echoed in my head when I walked the lonesome valley to church,
past nodding Zulu plumes of mighty toetoe,
while paspalum tassels played diminuendo;

then those clouds, that summer, and that milk bar,
whose classic ice-creams melted in double time:
golden hokey-pokey crumbled to sweet gritty bits.
From Beatle boots we graduated to the Twist.
Doorstop evangelists banged on about Judgement Day,
while farmers, the nation's backbone, were making hay.

Donovan it was who sang, Wear your love like heaven,
and I thought of him in Carnaby Street in turtleneck paisley
and corduroy loons, reeking of sage, thyme and parsley.
The Beach Boys went barbershop with hit parade tunes;
their 'Good Vibrations' theremin hummed and swooned.
Shiny grooves of LPs rippled on the turntable:
like a dark iron butterfly on a vanilla fudge wall.
I'm listening to Janis wail, Get it while you can,
and to Mister Mojo Rising, the Lizard King,
who broke on through Blake's Doors of Perception.
Martin Sharp covered Cream's double album in silver.
When boiled Cona coffee grounds simmer down,
the air-con still wafts cool from the mezzanine lounge,
all through 246 Queen Street up to His Lordship's.
On black and white TV, we watched *Town and Around*,
and Martin Luther King's mourners bearing witness.
San Francisco was where you wore flowers in your hair,
while Jefferson Airplane sang, Feed your head.

Love is everything, everything is nothing, hippies said;
acid soaked their world in hallucinogens:
hypnotic swirls, painted-on flowers, peace signs.
They groped for answers through hazy smokescreens,
in leather vests and handmade boots of buckskin.
On our school bus trip, we chanted, until
the packed bus boomed like the school's old PA —

Hey, hey, hey, LBJ, how many kids did you kill today?
And, two-four-six-eight, Pentagon levitate!
Jumping Sundays made Albert Park a Mecca,
as rebels swarmed up from damp villas,
jumped in the fountain, and protested War.
My hair shook, thick like a guardsman's shako.
Ponsonby's Progressive Youth hawked *Earwig* issues.
Ours not to do or die, but to smoke and stay high.
By Downtown Chemists, the Midnight Cowboy stands;
is that bomb, guitar or alarm clock in his hands?
He's wearing his Disraeli gears; he's waiting for Gobbo;
he is about the same as he was yesterday,
drowning his sorrows upstairs in Babel Café,
sharing poems with Hēmi, a barefoot bearded man,
who prays to be buried in olive-green tarp at Jerusalem.

## SEVEN OLD BASTARDS OF AUCKLAND

(after *Les Sept Vieillards*, by Charles Baudelaire)

Formication of ants, humid city with a skinful,
Where the drunkard from his beer garden stirs
To bail up the passer-by for dosh to go on the piss.
Ah, the Seventies, when rotgut flowed like seawater
In the mazy channels of the mud mangroves.

Quite early one morning the bards were at it,
In a booze barn on the street of sorrows,
As Rangitoto rolled to oarlock rattle
And pōhutukawa spat grog blossom on roads.

Rain held off like a shower of shit at milking,
As a cow-cockie might observe, scratching stubble,
And heated arguments rose from bungalows
Where families were going nuclear in the suburbs.

Suddenly a cove in ancient garb declaimed
From the back of a city-bound Railways bus I was on
Of the Throne and Gehenna and Ahab's bones,
As if fresh from a Gisborne whale stranding.

You would have thought his eyeballs had drowned in gin,
His gaze as hard as Jack Frost's in winter,
And his Rasta beard like rātā vines climbed his chin.
He wasn't bent but broken, like tōtara lightning-blasted,
And he leaned on a tokotoko walking stick,
And shouted to the driver to stop and let him off — yah prick.

When he climbed down, an overcoated twin followed him,
Holding a battered suitcase bound with baling twine.
The pair with tattered clothes and worn-out shoes
Were headed to the early opener at Ōtāhuhu.

This was the state of play back in the day,
When they still saluted at the RSA,
And there was more than one, there were more than two,
Of these professor longhairs squaring up for a boozaroo.

I counted them up everywhere, rub-a-dub-dub,
Seventy-seven times seven they crowded in,
Shoulder to shoulder at the urinals that passed for pubs.

Let those who laugh at my disquietude,
In these days of vapes and touchscreen japes,
Just think that despite so much decrepitude
From that schickered multitude, they owned the territory.

They were on the swag and welcome to prop up the bar.
They swayed, they crowed, they knocked them back,
They drank them down, they chundered Ruth!
And up Khyber Pass Road the brewery tills rang and rang.

## SMOKE

A burning wand wafts in plumes to be exhaled
in volcanic rush, smoke erupting from nostrils,
as if out of vents in the earth, only a devil's dream.

Unrepentant, gathered down alleys to blow smoke
each other's way: each cigarette marks time, ground
out like a coffin nail hammered to a coffin lid.

Each is weighty, a stoned idol, smoke issuing
from the mouth as swirls cast forth, containing
curative properties, powers to raise the dead.

Light my fire, give me a puff, and then burn
down the main drag: for the space of a smoke,
he was wheeling his helix towards eternity.

He smoked the Book of Genesis through prison,
page by page, and aimed a forefinger and thumb,
bang, bang, at the guards the length of his days.

He resembled a blackened smokestack city,
gritty of speech, burning tobacco at midnight,
in gardens of pleasure, till old with taste of ashes.

His smile crooked as a broke-down castle, he smoked
at warnings, the blighted gums and teeth on the pack,
his lower inside lip forever tattooed with *Ake! Ake!*

## Old School Prize

The timekeeper looks at my date stamp,
my damp pages stained brown as spilt tea
or weak coffee, and clocks my bent spine,
the dog-eared corners and wrinkled edges,
the fact that I've been on this back shelf
so long, since some time last century
would you believe: slim volume, old school prize,
inscribed, beaten up, dust jacket lost;
and places me in the box for worn-out cast-offs.

## ODE TO WEARY DUNLOP

I used to amble, I used to ankle, I'd hopscotch along.
I'd bop, I'd diddly-bop, I'd pad, I'd percolate through the throng.
In the disco, in the bistro, I'd get on shanks' pony,
and traipse it all night long.
And now it's the hesitation waltz, the blind bat foxtrot,
the yearning saunter, the excuse me after dark.
The shamble shanks, the slow bandy legs,
the disconsolate gesture is no walk in the park.
I can no longer yomp across shifting sands
as a riptide tugs quick at my heels,
I'm on the wagon, I'm on the shelf,
I'm looking forward to meals on wheels.
But to tramp and never tire of it,
breathing in jungle's penumbra at dusk,
like that colossus of rutted roads,
that Australian in his slouch hat,
with his remnant of juggernaut army,
that life-saving surgeon in charge
with his wry grin and his sloping brim.
To walk and never tire of it,
as Weary Dunlop never did,
his guidance an airstrip
in the jungle of the mind.
And so I stagger after never-weary Weary,
who had sandals made of old tyres,
and carried that scorched-earth smell of War,
drifting our way with the whirring
of propellers and flying-boat drone.
There were the Japs, and the other chaps,
up on the screen, with bayonets waved around,
POW camp barbed wire, David Niven with his frown.

Those feature flicks we watched agog,
before we played it out again on the rifle range
abandoned at the back of the Air Force base,
the sky dead calm with that heat haze,
as men went past in jeeps and sun-baked khaki.
When black and white ran in reverse,
divers burst out of the water backward,
arcing through air on to the springboard
of an amazingly blue swimming pool.
So here's to us now, soft tyres around the waist,
afloat on the vast white sarcophagi of cruise ships,
backpedalling through Asia in the slack season,
looking for the old Burma Railway
and finding the well-paved boulevard.
Things have changed for the better,
gone the forced march, the flogged march,
the sack race march, the dead march,
across an acreage of broken pedestals,
tireless as the ghost of Weary Dunlop,
whose men once shuffled forward
with the sad wallow of tyres gone flat.

## DEATH WARMED UP

Party, party, party — and amongst them walking, Mister Death.
Understand: he wants to be your bed companion,
But the door only swings one way for Mister Death.
Beneath the sun, Mister Death's a personality cult of none.
Death might parade naked for your delectation;
Camouflaged in articulation: a grinning skeleton.
Brought up in a moral vacuum, Death never says never.
Death preens from every mirror; grey panthers patrol the border.

Death, a gambler, stalks and skulks, punter to punter.
Death's nightmare in general is a fear of the funeral.
Yet, no matter how fast, Death comes gaining.
Death's hearse rolls up lickety-split; so, you must hop into it.
Some tussle; some holler; some fight; but all at last lie silent and still.
As, by your hand, Darkness leads you, Death keeps faith with Night.

## THE VALETUDINARIANS

Fallen-down butterfly town's torn and frail.
The farmhouse bends on crutches now.
The waterhole's a rock-filled begging bowl,
bared to what oven of baking sun will allow.
The rain-tanks, dry and rusted, whang like bullets.
The sheep are shorn, and long gone.
The hills slope away to steep ravines,
to the land of long Sunday afternoons and hedged bets.
Breezes bring retreat of the glaciers,
advance of the subdivision battalions.
On all the breezes, moths from pockets sail.
Evening light embronzes feather and fern.
Hear the call of the climb, the grunt of the scrum.
Like Charles Upham, plotting his escape
from Colditz, they gaze rum from backblocks:
for a coven of stooped valetudinarians,
the only way out is in a wooden box.

## Prayer for Rain

First on pavements, polka dots appear,
in steady tick-tock to pock dry ground;
tiny splashes that teem and mist the air.
Scrawl it in pencil, with tentative hand,
squint at its fume, its haze of distance;
Farmers, oilskin-clad, adopt a stance;
squinting upwards in a solemn band.
A stone church preens as the rain arrives;
with candles snuffed out, smell of petrichor.
Rain begins to throw its weight around.
Harbouring clouds bring their soakage:
water to glissade and dance in downpour.
It trip-hops, dub-steps, flails from eaves,
foams like champagne from popped corkage.
Big drops curve to lobes that spill from trees.
Let rain weep, blub, gurgle, what it believes;
it swirls, it sculls, it launches a stampede;
a last round-up with thunder and drums.
From blinked smirr to the din of cataract,
never disdain to feel and taste fresh rain.
It'll pat you down, surround, and even drown.
Every pane of glass that's touched is tracked,
as streaks of moisture sidle sideways,
blown in triumph from a far corner
of the sky, where they first kept hidden,
stashed and stowed amongst drab vapour.
On tyre skim, a nimbus shine tells
of roads black as submerged mussel shells.
Park up beneath dripping fern fronds
to watch run-off make tar-seal ponds.
Backyards brim with sopping fennel,

long grass might be wrung like laundry.
In early hours we hear such heavy rains
gush through the rough-and-tumble of drains.
Rains sound in chorus, sudden and slow,
or high and faint, or deep and low.
Rains will drench, then are hardly there.
Far away, streams go coursing along
to form a cadence chant of river-song,
or else pool and darken in a mountain tarn.
Those afternoons of rain being recollected;
when I'm right as rain, rains make strange;
beyond house windows, their ghosts estrange.
For in the drought we pray for rain, and curse
seven days later when it hasn't stopped.

## MURIWAI, TE HENGA, ANAWHATA, PIHA, KAREKARE

Haloed by squalls ferny steeps trickle.

Nīkau's green spears shake off drizzle.

Gulls stalk fizz of damp black grains.

Over velvet footprints shallows sidle.

Rollers crash where stingray shades float.

Bubbles wreathe foam's silky prisms.

Bladderwrack tentacles flex their gloss.

Small frogs slide through bush pockets.

Five gannets stitch the sky in single line.

## ISTHMUS

Sugar Town's rush hour fills choke points below
the biggest exclamation mark on death row,
concrete hypodermic lit by gamble fever,
the watchtower needle struck by weather.
Kite flying in forked lightning, ant trails,
skull headlands whose houses gleam gold teeth:
I nibble at the corners of dark cloud reef.
Woks singed over flames in food halls;
white pelts fur gutters after hail falls.
Forklifts carry pallets, and engines growl;
off hot pavements steam plumes; high heels clatter.
Yellow petals tumble in memorial gardens;
a mānuka bud is a song in the city of sails.
The siren calliope serenades harbour mermaids;
anorexic spectres waver in door plate glass.
Lights, a pimple rash on pinched neck of isthmus:
the container ship glides under blood-orange moon.

## AT THE CAFÉ

Consumers near-by wallow
in tubs of pink strawberry slush,
possibly with added corn syrup and palm oil.
I'm here, I'm here at the café,
with the achingly hip,
their cappuccino froth angst,
their long black thoughtfulness,
their genteel flat white slurp,
their repressed scrabble for a banished cigarette,
their screen-glow of imminent selfie-hood.
They might sky-write with a vape pen in a snow globe.
And soon I'll be making knee-jerk reflex pieties,
down the aisles of a printed paper cathedral,
on my way to the next book festival.

## Portrait of the Artist

They're thrown the Bauhaus under an electric bus.
They've torn a strip off Mondrian's downtown bougie-woogie.
They've reinvented Malevich's black square as a Rubik's Cube.
They've turned Joseph Beuys into a wet blanket the size of the Beehive.
They've stuck glitter and metallics all over the sackcloth and ashes.
They've travelled on a shoestring, carrying a Barry Brickell bowl.
They've cancelled the Colin McCahon stamps.
They've woken up the Len Lye sculpture.
They've planted Billy Apple in the Karl Maughan garden.
They've gone to a far-out galaxy of art collectives.
They've become a conceptual ambassador for an Australian bank.
They've become a pinball wizard with a spray-can.
They've become a smoke alarm, emitting faint beeps of distress.
They're covered all over by an Onehunga onesie.

## POSSUM THE POET

Possum the Poet reclines in a tree
to watch hordes of rabbits run free,
and hears a voice behind the shelter belt
yell, Get out of it! to a sheep dog
worrying a skinned carcass,
wanting guts for garters,
as keen sounds sharpen and prick up ears.
Possum writes an ode to what
eight out of nine possums
chose as their final meal,
and another that addresses
those skeletal trees which hold
mummified remains of possums.
When Possum's cranium's full of grubs,
and poison has got his goat,
he'll be blued with 1080,
and contorted, a crucified possum,
from the crossbar of a goalpost.
Till then, he'll doss down on a part of the farm,
where Enoch Axeman has left his chopped-up frown.

## Logo Daedalus

Bell, book and candle will cast their spell.
Logo Daedalus is a witching creation.
They don't mince words, where words spring from;
but we will make them eat their cake.
They may bamboozle, with petty flapdoodle;
but we can put words up against the wall,
blindfold, execute, drag them out by their boot heels.
Big words, small words, twenty-four-dollar words.
Roll them up, like cannabis leaf, to smoke.
There are words of deceit, words that bring grief,
words wanting one last throw of the dice.
Disruptive, unspeakable words, just not very nice.
Words that make their way towards us, solemn
and devout, but that only want us
to buy into their users' lures and wares.
Sensations become words in desperation
to be heard, to make some noise in the void.
Words whirl away in a torn-up flurry.
Uttered words come back to me in reverse order,
and very slowly I take apart words' mystery,
till I stand stock-still in the middle of empty.

## THE GREAT NEW ZEALAND NOVEL

I went looking for the Great New Zealand Novel,
I searched high and low, and into every hovel.
I hungered for the grizzle, for the nudge of a sheep dog's muzzle,
for *The Bone People*, for *Owls Do Cry*,
for *The God Boy* and *The Godwits Fly*,
for *Plumb* and *Paddy's Puzzle*,
for *Among the Cinders* and *The Hole in the Zero*,
for *The Vintner's Luck* and *All Visitors Ashore*,
for *Came a Hot Friday* and *The Luminaries*;
for all those novels that were testifying histories.
Novels with their feathered sandals and houghmagandie scandals,
novels with their French letters and nutty professors,
novels with their peripheral vision of Christ risen,
novels with their dust jackets of distinction,
novels that chug like post-colonial post-hole borers
deep into the sediment of sentiment.
I sought novels that don't skite, that don't get too flash,
novels in praise of the California bungalow or 'Pōkarekare Ana',
novels where the wheels are coming off the Junketville minibus,
novels that feature some philosopher-king of the backblocks,
two-fisted and Hemingwayesque and quite grotesque,
novels where not a lot happens very slowly,
novels that mooch along apologising as they go,
novels from way back when the pub was an unreconstructed chauvinist piggery,
novels that preserve the decorum of the creative writing class
nuzzling rather than biting the hand that feeds,
novels able to grab hold of the zeitgeist
and swing it by the tail over the wall and out,
novels at once salacious, loquacious and ludicrous,
wearing an air of bogus profundity and little else,
novels forever blowing soap-opera bubbles,

novels that, instead of dancing about in the voluminous skirts
of a hand-me-down Victorian fustian like a kind of precocious drag act,
or parading about in the pleated and ironed army khaki
of the Sons of Sargeson and associated epigoni,
are written in the over-caffeinated staccato
of an author hiding in a witness-relocation programme.
I went looking for the Great New Zealand Novel,
I looked high and low, I went to Central Otago
and to Balclutha in the snow, to the rhododendron dell in Karori
where the ghost of Katherine Mansfield was said to dwell,
in a zombie novel, or was KM the spirit of the Napier Soundshell?
I came across novels characterised by a chatty volubility,
and other novels rigid with defensive irony,
novels highly homogenous and dreary,
and yet other novels quite anti-imperialistic.
There were novels written in a childishly simple diction,
and one or two exploding like joke cigars
with a fraction too much cultural friction,
while some had people come and go for no discernible reason
in settings that were difficult to determine.
They all made claims to be the Great New Zealand Novel,
and even if those claims were hollow or atrocious,
I was no longer sure that I would recognise the Great New Zealand Novel,
even if it came up to me wearing an expression quite ferocious,
because does a novel really require such evaluation,
when all are engaged in writing one single Great Novel of the nation?

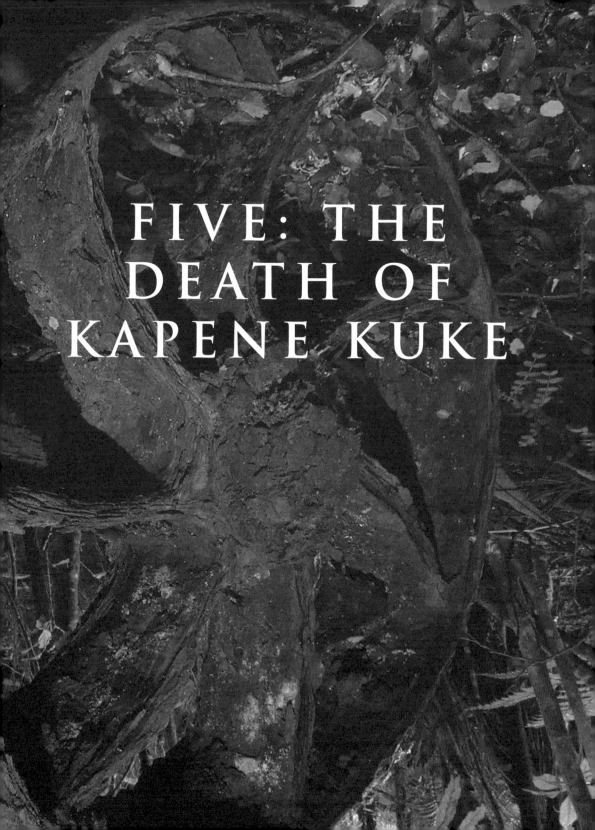

# FIVE: THE DEATH OF KAPENE KUKE

# The Death of Kapene Kuke

Burning holes of Pele's eyes are witness.
Floating islands glide, planted with slender
and tall trees that are slung with wind-catchers.
A shark hula dances from island to island,
green peaks rise like dorsal fins of sailfish.

Haku Mele the chant-master calls ancestors;
umbilical cords bind us to the earth.
Kapene Kuke the skydiver walks
amongst us, celebrated with flower garlands,
but desecrates tapu when sailors take
rails for firewood and trample temple grounds.

Was Kuke a god? Lono-makua, his rain-keeper?
No, Kuke was not a god; he deceived the people.
Abstracted, careless, Kuke misunderstood all.
At Makahiki, to the thudding of drums,
dawn from its pit of fire is ascending
lighting domains of clouds, currents, blue swells.

Kanaka was beaten by Kuke's sailors, so stole
a boat, then broke it up for nails for fishhooks.
Kuke went to take the paramount chief
hostage. The people stopped him, and Kuke
was clubbed and stabbed. Mother Pele's anger
shone red lava through air, earth and water.

With hiss and crack waves sizzled on hot rock,
as Kuke fell from black lava at Kealakekua Bay.
Pele, goddess of the volcano, turned as cold
as a lei in a United States refrigerator,

and rains stirred, awakening the war god's rhythms.
Kūkā`ilimoku is eater of islands,
swallows them greedily in a shroud of bubbles.

Kuke was washed and wrapped in taro leaves,
then laid in a shallow pit sprinkled with sand,
and a fire burned over his body for ten days.
Freed from flesh, his scorched bones were gathered,
wrapped in kapa cloth and placed in the temple.

Kuke's heart was hung up in a fern hut,
where it was found and devoured by children
who mistook it for the heart of a dog.
Warriors diced for his bones, whittled away
as relics taken for spears and fishhooks,
though some were retrieved by Kuke's sailors,
and consigned to the deep wrapped in canvas.
Kapene Kuke died for the handful of nails
that held a cutter together. Captain
Cook brought capitalism and Adam Smith's saws,
rather than reciprocity and sharing of gifts,
and he was not the great white god Lono,
but one speared through and smoked till flesh seared off,
as the rain dogs ran with the grey rain gods.

Kapene Kuke shot a man who threw a spear,
with his double-barrelled gun, but the man
was wrapped in layers of wet kapa cloth
and so bullet-proof; each musket ball rebounded
and fell, harmless. Then another man struck,
and another, before Kuke tumbled into the sea.
Someone wanted the hallowed slab on which Cook
made his last stand blasted out and taken to America

as Exhibit A; instead, Hawai`i
itself was stolen to become the fiftieth state.

## HONOLULU BY NIGHT

*WrestleMania* watched day by day
made him what he is — a rock and roller.
And then, next minute, he's that tar-baby,
suddenly finding that someone has set fire
to him at midnight. He was sticky pitch,
and up it ran, a stream of orange flame.
In his own mirror he was the very portrait
of a serial killer, for he killed himself over
and over. He found his own beach and beached
there. It was all sand dune; hands stuck inside
garbage bins and held tight by the handshake
of melted plastic. He was washed out to sea
with a hose. In the wash, there were too many
like him to count, clinging to their phones
as if they might be life rafts, and text
made flesh as a sashimi platter. What lies
beyond the great green curtains of jungle?
More blue, more blue, through the mountains
and through the crater, through the lava tubes,
and all through the coral brain that pulses to reef fish flitter.

# WAITING FOR HURRICANE LANE

In a Honolulu diner before the hurricane,
I am a big fan, all blades whirring,
of Mexican ode poet Tabasco,
so fiery, so spicy, so bitter, so sweet —
senses compounded in one salt sob.
I hiccup verbs, peppery with heat,
confronted by fragrant tumble-down flowers
yellow in blue sky glare, tropic bowers
flashing like a mariachi band serenading,
or a machete band harvesting sugar cane.

Swish, swish, swish goes the ceiling fan,
steel brushes sounding on a snare drum.
Coffee fountains from Americano valves.
Nets dredge sea beds to plonk contents
gasping in the dark hold of Waikiki buses,
watertight compartments in submarine dive.
Pidgin vocabularies confound a slow-
moving traffic cha-cha with brazen horns.
Sidewalks trickle with torrid sweatiness,
through snail-smeared barometric dawn.

Cast-off cloth unbound, we clap hosannahs,
hail the new thing, doff baseball caps for old.
And surfers are summoned to snowy hills
become liquid, where caps toss adrift in loss.
Giraffe towers sway their hotel balconies.
Hurricane Lane gathers ballooning clouds,
butterflies, graveyards of microplastic.
The airborne Pacific Garbage Patch might fall
skull-and-crossboned on sunken navy ships,
and chase frail white egrets to skulk inland.

Wind wobbles a moped rider's hand-held ladder,
and the singing sirens of aimless ambulances.
TV's 'Lane' might be the revolving eye of a god,
bringing rain heavy as fists, leaving bruises.
I'm aghast at this forecast violent hurricano,
this pressure drop, apocalyptic slam dunk;
but what we get is only wild wind rush,
a moody wind-shear waterdrop slash-slash,
and howls like orphans, widows, sisters sinister,
all the trees bucking like rodeo horses.

Resonances rumble, distant as whale song.
Each bamboo stand is bent in a tight knot.
Places are shuttered, their doors slammed taut.
They look almost vacant. Busy spaces bolted.
The wind yahoos and whistles; things clang.
Pebbles, flung up, shy against leprous walls.
The building where we lodge wheezes then gasps,
lurching on its foundations. Each room booms.
Waves from far away surge like shock troops.
Banshees on roofs rap out weird mating calls.

At last, downtown's freed by rainbow's shine
from you desperado monster of weather,
a broken-up, foggy, nightmare dreamboat,
that took Hawai`i by its gurgling throat.
Yet your drops still bead me with tendrils,
and so I am prompted to pelagic memories.
My mind has the eye of a hurricane
at the centre, and the eye of the hurricane
has a drone at the centre, and the drone has
a mind at the centre, heading for open ocean.

## NIGHT FISHING

Mischievous chop of waves,
sweetened by ukulele strums.
The day's blue wings align;
blackness, freckled with gold.
Night ink's perfect musk;
a decoy bobs, and the fish
is gone with a splash,
lifted flapping into the boat.

## Plumeria Flowers

Summer's frangipani
drifts between branches;
sunshine in my veins
sings out with joy.

## LIFTING THE ISLAND

Virtuous sunlight lifts the island to prayer.
The abyss is dizzyingly blue to dive into.
Surfers are carried on the backs of waves.
Hotels rear balcony totems notched skyward.
Heat yawns with a reptile's tranced shimmer.
Dazzled clouds somersault; then roll away,
from a day flapping in an ocean breeze.

Girls in just bikinis and flip-flops,
their long hair streaming in the wind,
weave mopeds and surfboards beachwards,
listening to iTunes, white buds in their ears,
flat out in heavy traffic, as fat men
on fatter hogs roar along with the racket
of low-flying, propeller-driven, fighter planes.

The beachcomber who once sailed seven seas,
goes from bin to bin with freestyle hands,
grave as a mandarin in abstract thought.
Ripe stink of garbage. Hot weeks of August.
He wears nothing but faded and ripped shorts,
his muscles ripple under sun-blackened skin,
his fingers toil to free mashed drink cans.

The old gods are curios, remade in the bar
as the grinning wooden handles of beer taps.
Those at the bar, heads bowed, dream of surf,
dream of white foam swept into a cold glass.
Fleeting moments woven like flower garlands,
a seaweed hula undulating in a ship's wake.
The howl of air-con strains to cool down rooms.

Catch the smoking wave on winged heels,
orchidaceous comber that lifts rose-gold,
before deep green, light green, greener, bluer,
deeper, darker, roller-slider rising, standing,
before weight of water beneath the rolling
wave topples to wipe out, because the sea
has been stopped by land shelving beneath.

# THE SHARK-HULA DANCER

A coral reef hardens to atolls,
and lava climbs from seawater,
so grasp the cloak of feathers and leap
to dark-barked cloud, where mists
are carved into swirls, or woven
into strands that reach down to islands.

Fleet as a flying fish through the surf
pursued by sharks below and birds above,
the shark-hula dancer rides wave's glare,
till opaque rain quenches sun's sear.
Ride that hyperbolic wave to `Ohana, where
the whānau braid and rebraid forever.

Shine, dolphins in pods, orchestras of stingrays,
flying fish and swimming birds arrayed,
as tidebeat's endless azure washes over.
When you die, your conch trumpet will be buried
beneath hot lava flowing from Kīlauea,
while spirals tighten and snow falls on Mauna Loa.

## TOURIST ISLAND

I swam with the turtles, with the military,
under paddle boards, within earshot of pickets
beating on buckets and chanting for equity.

Those church bells that toll in black and white,
they anger the sea. On its back rolls a whale,
to sink under in calm daylight.
The sea now is just recycled fishing nets,
microplastics in a gyre, doing figure-of-eights.

Carved, wooden, I face towards the gleams.
I face towards translucent shallows.
I worship the idol, its fabric scraps
that the naked sea covers and swallows.
The sea holds a mirror to its own reflections
in silver, and thrusts me under as distortions.

I'm mesmerised by the sunshine's sheen,
and every minute particular feels like mine.

The sea disgorges its catalogue of shells
on the white page of sand for no one.

On my hotel bed, I dream and sail.

## THROW NET

Everything spoken whirrs as a wheel.
A fire truck vibrates in its crabshell.
Surf tumbles storms of white petals.

The yellow flame of the bamboo cane
licks up all the afternoon rain,
to feed the green smoke of its leaves.

The snores of a sleeper on a beach towel
recite genealogy under volcano's glow.
A sunken raft of manta rays stirs after dark.

Hands hula-hula, shaping sandwiches
into islands; mechanically, a shark
takes a bite out of the moonlight.

Someone slings a hammock between trees.
Each wave is a line; each line is breaking;
and even the mountains are setting sail.

## ON O`AHU

Around the island, you rode the bus,
and by so doing lit up the compass,
till petrol-tainted you almost fainted,
as old Chinatown steamed with ancient rains.
In perpetual merry-go-round, curses sound,
behind grilles, grates and iron bars,
as a fierce heat strikes like eagle claws.
Asphyxia of the all, and smell of the Fall,
brings hired actors in crime scene enactments.
He's strung up by his bootlaces in a windowless
holding room with no metal fixtures,
after sleepwalking through town high on sirens.
Elderly, she's looking to have work done,
then voting for picture-perfect oblivion.
Sportcasters, overheard, pontificate split hairs;
Supreme Beings are drinking Bud Light beers.
Educated by cathode ray back in the day,
now we read the internet to forget.

Underneath, the rainbow tastes of egg yolk;
shaved ice lime runs its song along my tongue.
A skull glitters in diamonds on a stick pin;
take a candy cane and go surf street din.
Baked by sun, skin sucks in the prize it won.
Mud-crabs fret the mud for a salty lark;
broken nets entwine shoreline by the park.
Life-change channel, a remote you can afford,
along with canoe paddle and ironing board.

## WAIKIKI, O`AHU

Red zone, green zone, blue zone, street zone, food zone, bed zone, dead zone, as if looking round cloud nine, seventh heaven, some resort island, or some slum, where the poor live, and dream of owning something larger than themselves. The suntanned rough sleeper sits cross-legged on his traffic island, complete with coconut palm. The bearded rough sleeper in a blanket lies flat along the bench at a bus stop. The manic pram-pusher, whose baby buggy contains only a loaded boom-box blasting rap music, hurries, skittering along, but stops to dole out a couple of dollar bills to each rough sleeper, fishing in a clutter of plastic bags tied to the pram handles, and the day is as dry as hot sand grains blown in from the beach two blocks away.

The man paralysed from the neck down steers his electric wheelchair on to the bus-door ramp, and down the street. He trundles a block or so to his busker's pitch on the boulevard next to Waikiki Beach. He stops first at a bike shop, where the friendly manager helps him drape the set of small bells around his neck and over one arm that he then jiggles to make delicate music. His Stetson hat that travels on top of the canopy over his wheelchair is now on the pavement in front of him, and here is where this wheelchair-bound performer will remain all morning, his jingle of bells competing with the roar of refrigerated ice-cream trucks, the clatter of open-sided tourist trolley buses and the clamour from Sheraton Hotel workers on strike further along the road, using megaphones and steadily banging on drums.

## LIFE LESSONS

Change your currency to change your life.
Take up with Indigo Slam,
leave your boyfriend a skeleton.
Let it all turn to custard and start over.
First, kill all the lawyers,
then kill your darlings,
and if you meet the Buddha
on the road, kill him.
Toke the dried venom
of the Sonoran Desert toad.
Be brah on a weed jag,
on the second morning joe,
as surfing birds blow smoke
up the Banzai Pipeline.
Lay down track marks,
lay down white line fever,
go crossing against the traffic,
let your kite catch the wind,
up, up and away.
Dip toenails, rake fingers, comb back locks.
Nebulous, pursue a chimera
through Pearl Harbor.
Hit a steel drum pan roll.
Ride a souped-up wheelchair.
When they put it on you
to cross the t's and dot the i's,
have your papers in order in a safe house,
be ready for the firestorm.

## United States Flag, Hawai`i

Power of the flag in the wind,
wrapped around itself, shaken
free and rippled out again,
charging along on air, electric.

American antlers, American war bonnets,
American smoke signals, a butchered carcass,
then thousands more, what a cacophony!
Metallic cries, raucous vibes, red polls.

Once below a time, when your mind is flat
and you've retired exhausted from all avenues,
ask yourself, why learn history
when my phone does that for me?

I am the dark backward abysm.
I am a form of extreme conservatism.
I am the boulevard nobody knows.
I smell not of a rose is a rose is a rose,
but of sick and bitter residues of the sea.

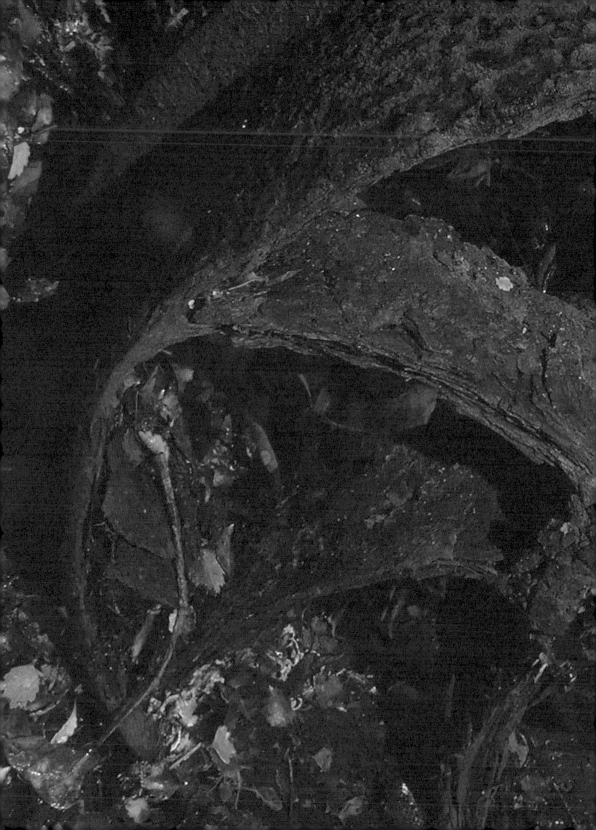

# SIX: WHALE SONG

## WHALE SONG

Talitali fiefia to whales of Vava`u, under red moon, hinehina rainbow, radiance
of Māhina, soft rains of `Ua. Malo `aupito to tofūa`a hamupaká: the humpback
whales, big swimmers through all colours of the ōseni — lanu pulū, lanu mata,
lanu panefunefu. Time slows at sea-level and sinks in bubbles. Fạiåkse`ea to
vaka-tonga, journeying to outer islands over teeming realms of Tagroa, reaching
to hanuạ of Rotuma. Noa`ia `e mauri, praise to your bounty, Tagroa: flying fishes,
great whales leaping in spray and mist. Beyond the horizon, winds are talking,
calling to spirits. Each atua is in balance; the whales are singing.

# Te Ara-a-Parāoa, Path of the Sperm Whale

Aotearoa's white peaks spyhop above waves,
seeking albatross worlds of mislaid moons.
Screeching kākā skim fast through treetops.
Parāoa breaches in a frost-smoke chrysalis.
Iwi on the shore perform haka of welcome.
Drizzle dances on the head of the whale.
Hoisted up out of water, blowing a guffaw,
headlands slap and wallow in their turn.
A living wall slides past, gentle-eyed, vast.
Luminous planktons glow in ocean darkness;
neon flying squid flash through salty air.
Silvery-bubbled, ripple-guided, Parāoa
tilts her tail-flukes, keels and plunges:
guiding her calf down Kaikōura Canyon.
Bob of a fur seal pup snouts through
seaweed wrack, in the surf's long swell.
A breeze licks over spun gobbets of foam.
A green tendril climbs sunwards in a spiral.

## THE DREAM OF THE HUMPBACK WHALE

I'm a humpback whale, my dream is to fly.
Blunt-nosed and blubbery I may be,
but my blowhole jets out sea-spray proudly.
I am buoyant with air, and go under the waves.
I carry my bulk with delicate ease.
My head is covered with bumps, knobs, barnacles,
but I have long flippers, at least five metres,
and with these I can make a lot of noise.
My whale spirit flies above in the gulls' cries.
I furrow low in the water like a thrillseeker.
I scull backward, and upward, to go forward.
A behemoth grey and white, as big as a bus,
I break out of the brine, I'm reaching high.
I hurtle over the fishes, I startle the turtles,
and try to catch the eye of any passer-by,
as I make boat hulls rock with a mighty splash.
I'm dramatic, I'm acrobatic, I'm ecstatic.
I leap then fall like a skydiver on fast forward.
I'm a dancing god, doing a hornpipe jig.
I desire to go where my wing-like flukes will not fail.
I'll eat the equator, and breathe in the sky;
be the humpback whale who sails through the gale.
I'll surface in soft rains to dance in the bay,
and chase down the whalers of days gone by.

## THE INNER HARBOUR

The pygmy blue whale comes by, off-shore.
The dwarf minke whale comes by, off-shore.
The pygmy right whale comes by, off-shore.
They make their way into the inner harbour,
past the pear trees, the hills and the houses,
past where King Shag commands the view,
past where the twisted rātā flowers on cliff-tops;
as saltwater flows into the channels of the harbour,
as ribbons of kelp sway in the crystal of the harbour,
as white seabirds hover over the oyster-grey harbour;
till all is swept up on the coastal high tide,
before each whale floats out on the coastal ebb tide,
swimming away from the seaweedy harbour;
and a tsunami's faint ripples finally arrive
from far-flung Vanuatu, west of Fiji,
across Te Moana-nui-a-Kiwa, the great ocean of Kiwa;
and silvery beams of moonlight waver on waves.
See the sky brushed thick with stardust,
see the stars, tapu stars, little star eyes of Matariki,
the whetū mārama, the whetū moana,
all the stars in the sky without number,
the large stars, the small stars, the stars red and yellow;
all the bright stars of Rangi the Sky-father;
see the bright stars, against the Void of Te Kore.

## ORCAS

Hail to the orca, carnivore, apex predator.
We are killer whales from Antarctica.
We like it cold because then we go fast,
under the icebergs, beneath polar winds.
Listen to the icepack grind; listen to gales moan.
Hail to the orca, carnivore, apex predator.
We click and we trill to communicate.
We are orcas, we pulse with sonic power:
pods that whistle together stay together.
We move through the sea with flabbergasting speed.
We slide over ice floes to snatch up penguins.
We snap giant petrels right out of the air.
We hunt sharks, rays, sealions, dolphins;
we toss them and tumble them and gulp them down.
Hail to the orca, carnivore, apex predator.
We like it cold, because then we go fast.
When fish dart and veer, they know death is near.
We're black on top with white behind our dorsal fin,
and when we get encrusted with algae, with diatoms,
that create too much drag and slow us down,
we cross the ocean, fast as we can to warmer seas,
and only there in the tropics do we shed our outer skin,
because we're warm-blooded and would otherwise freeze.
And then we race to the cold latitudes, all shiny and new,
back to where the icebergs glitter in the sun.
We whoop and we hunt and we travel as one.
We are orcas, carnivores, apex predators.
We are killer whales from Antarctica.

## THE NAVIGATORS

Our outriggers sailed to archipelagos
    – carrying fishhooks
    – carrying taro seedlings
    – carrying gourds of rainwater.
We navigated
    – by shapes and colours of clouds
    – by behaviour of birds
    – by smell of plants and seaweed.
We steered at night
    – by moon and stars,
and on the darkest nights
    – by wind on our faces
    – by waves under the soles of our feet.
We tacked away
    – from waterspouts stirred up by gods
    – from flashes of distant lightning flung by gods
    – from sleet and ice reaching down from the realm of gods.
We chanted
    – to pumice rafts born in undersea furies.
We chanted
    – in storms to raised oar and furled sail-mat.
We chanted
    – through heat-haze to the basking turtle-sun.

We glided as the frigatebird glides,
to a rising atoll, until the atoll burst into leaf.
We chanted to Tagaloa, god of the sea,
as Tafola, the whale, breached beside us,
and guided us through the reef,
and then `ei reached out to lei
in a green cluster of atolls.

Our hulls sliced across the moana,
weaving together sprinkled islands,
low on the horizon;
awaiting a wave the height of a mountain,
dark blue beyond the reef in primal shimmer;
for life is an ocean wave,
from the creation of the world,
from the time of A`a, te atua, the gods,
from the time of kū`auhau, whakapapa, genealogy.

And now our island soil, torn up,
is flung skywards to hang suspended, trailing roots,
surrounded by empty ocean, vacuumed of fish.
And now we stand on our island,
chest-deep in the ocean, as the levels keep rising.

## TE WHEKE

Eight arms of Wheke connect a sea of islands.
But where does the head of Wheke lie?
Some say at Savai`i, some say at Hawai`i,
some say at Avaiki, some say at Tahiti.
In the strange deep dark where Wheke lives,
his long arms wind and curl far over the sea bed.
The drifting mass of Wheke has no fixed shape.
His eight suckered limbs undulate like flames.
His body can fit through a gap as wide as his eye.
He can look like a flounder or a sea-snake.
He has no stable texture, but unfurls in patterns.
His three hearts pump blue-green blood.
In an ocean with too many gods to count,
Wheke lives, rich, inky, and many-coloured.
His colours can enfold atolls in a blue mantle,
as Rā the-sun-god polishes across the moana.
From Nauru to Palau, Tuvalu to Vanuatu,
from Aitutaki to Mururoa, Tongatapu to Rapa Nui,
Wheke, the Giant Pacific Octopus, feels his way.
Above him is the ancient va`a Māhina-i-te-puna,
with a bow-wave that's flowering into white foam,
and whales are basking in all the anchorages.

# KĪLAUEA, THE BIG ISLAND

When akua Pele is blowing hot,
garlands of fire form on Kanaloa.
Pele's magma hisses like a dragon,
molten, bright as tropic flowers,
snowflakes settle on forest trees.
Today, a scroll of green fern shelters
delicate orchids, beyond black lava
slapped by wind and glare. In steam,
rainbow bubbles slide and burst.
The volcano smoulders and waits.
Pupualenalena broods in a boulder,
while netherworld 'aumākua seethe.
Magma, settled to hot mess gone cold,
to rivers of solid lava, has weathered
shiny and smooth. Crack it open,
you can see where sticky lava
has hardened into brittle layers;
it splinters, wafer-like, with air cells.
Along verges of cracked asphalt
roads around slumbering Kīlauea,
those dried wisps of lava flutter
to tell you the whole island is alive,
and when it stirs, and its fire erupts
through vents to plunge into the sea,
sending up hissing plumes of steam,
echoes will roar from other craters;
whales will be swimming for dear life.

## WHALE ROAD

I have seen harpoons glide while whales slept,
but now the whales are surging through,
energy dynamos in the ocean blue,
Bodhisattvas and protectors, guardians of the sea.
The whales carry the island, the whales carry every island.
follow the way of the whales, the whale road.
Where whales journey, people follow.
We follow the flow of the whales through open ocean,
we follow where the whale road goes.
The whales are wayfinders for our vaka,
the whales are wayfinders for our life raft,
for our dinghy, for our yacht, for our ferry, for our peace ship,
for our trawler, for our migrant boat, for our cruise ship,
for our container ship, for our oil tanker, for our naval ship —
and underneath them all, the holy holy holy whale swims.
We voyagers drift into the chop, into the azimuth,
into the girdle, into the circle, where all the winds blow.
Step aboard the old gospel ship, the Jonah boat,
with a creak and a shiver away to sea,
the sun has reached its zenith and we must follow —
the holy holy holy whale swims underneath them all,
through moon mist, loomings, starry darkness,
follow the whale's trail, follow the whales,
the whales are surging through.
Om mani padme hum.

## Whale in Rain: A Proverb from Rotuma

The rain has been falling all day,
and a whale serene,
in slow motion, slips through the marine,
massive, eerie, sublime;
moving through wave troughs,
under the roll of white-caps.
This is the time of `Ua-roa, the long rain,
falling on the fertile heart of the ocean,
made melancholy by the heavy rain.
So behold the whale,
surfacing slowly in the mournful rain,
rain that shrouds and shadows the ocean.
But the rain will stop some time;
no storm lasts forever:
E le`e se `ua e tōtō ai.

## WHALE TALK

Anchors away, ahoy, ahoy,
let us now praise the whale.
Slap your tail in the shallows, whale,
make the good times roll.
Shake shakers from shark-egg cases,
make the good times roll.
With a yo-ho-ho on a cask of rum,
there they blow, one by one,
make the good times roll.
Fifteen whales on a dead man's chest,
way on down in Davy Jones's locker,
make the good times roll.
Let it hum on the whale's eardrum,
make the good times roll.
Wallow once more in a calm swell,
let the whole world go to hell,
make the good times roll.
Where the whale goes, there go I,
along the wind, merrily,
make the good times roll.
All around a green agenda,
all through a blue abyss,
mā `ohi nui, with Pacific compass,
make the good times roll.
Wave crests shine white as ghosts,
under a hula-hula moon,
make the good times roll.
Grinning teeth beyond the reef,
dumped by far-out breakers,
make the good times roll.
Howzit braddah whale, mahola,

`ofa atu, hanisiof, talking story,
make the good times roll.
Glide on past sailfish crests,
when sea creeps in, sea creeps out,
when sea crawls up, sea crawls back,
make the good times roll.
Whale is the comfort animal of Kanaloa,
spirit of the planetary waves,
make the good times roll.
Slap your tail in the shallows, whale,
then slap your tail out at sea,
to boom-boom surf in the sacred dawn,
make the good times roll.

# ENDANGERED OCEAN BLUES

We all need to be humble before the whale, such beauty,
the biggest brain on the planet;
but seams are bulging with plastic
in the belly of the whale.
The sea is crapulous with mercury, phosphate, lead;
whales swim through big oil's leavings.
What will become of us without the whales?
The whales haunt us with their miseries;
they suckle their calves in distress;
so grieve for the sickness of the sea,
for it is the sickness of you and me,
eating ourselves to death in our billions,
chopping ourselves up for status symbols,
for nurdles, for tiny pieces of tomorrow.
Please believe, we are on the eve of extinction.
These are replicas of dead seas of the moon,
going extinct, extinct in the wild, vulnerable.
All, all are nearly gone, the old familiar creatures,
just their computer-generated features
remain; and the microtones of microplastics,
that scratch and scritch like a cracked recording,
spinning the resounding silence of the deeps,
where ghost-fishing by lost nylon walls-of-death
goes on for sailfish, swordfish, and marlin,
the fastest fish in the sea;
only there's no fish in the sea,
just whale-fall, the weight of dead whales down below.
The sea-green incorruptible has been corrupted:
over-fished, over-warmed, over-acidic;
and there, turning and turning in a gyre,
the endless dragnet of plastic.

## WHALE PSALM

The whale, says Jonah, is the black night filled with terrible screams.
The whale is missiles that winnow the grain from the wheatfields.
The whale is the city with bombed-out basements and burning high-rises.
The whale is the country, bogged down in booby traps and wreckage of tanks.
The whale shoulders the load, a tower of coffins.
The whale is village fiddlers tuning up a death march.
The whale is soldiers shouting their poems in the ruins.
The whale is a prayer on the lips of children.
The whale is liberty pecked at by birds of prey.
The whale is the enemy, with its taboos, its vanity and its ignorance.
The whale is life incarnate and a desperation to survive.
The whale is the weight of creation stranded on the tipping point.
The whale is always further away than first thought, but inescapable.
The whale wants to save us.
The whale wants to win the war.
The whale turns the spotlight on the whale-hunters and the war generals.
The whale has climbed the diving board above the dried-up sacred fountain.
The whale must dive into the circus barrel, and there is no way out.

# SEVEN: THE WALL

# The Wall

Because it's there, Mallory.
These, and all our rough notes, must tell the tale —
that we knocked the bastard off,
then split for Tranquility Base.
Everywhere the glint of gold,
wonderful things —
but time to pull finger, because more
will mean worse,
and I must get out of these clothes and into a dry ginger ale.
Yes, any colour, so long as it's black.
They are crying all the way to the bank,
they are going to spend, spend, spend.
Damn you, one percenters:
every other millimetre fool's gold,
at the thirteenth hour on the thirteenth day
of the thirteenth month.
Cast and recast as an angler at the lake of darkness,
leave your caste as one who misspoke, then woke.
Who goes as a joke?
He never kept his promise to build the wall,
greater than the Persian Gulf, the Great Wall of China,
the firewall of the Pentagon, the Berlin Wall,
the wall against Mexico, the West Bank Wall —
a wall the size and weight of Manhattan,
or a trillion dropped dimes.
Holy moolah was falling peacefully,
the TV quietly blinked and bled.
I never get out of bed
for less than the price on my head.
The engine idled and then it roared
with all its horsepower; it wouldn't be ignored.

The leaf blower rocked and rolled
every leaf to its appointed place.
A shower of rebate coupons fell in a field.
The heartland is a target poster drilled with bullets
that tourists fly over,
and the only thing growing is private prisons.
Put a frame around it and put on the orange jumpsuit.
Forget all those imaginary islands
where Havana is smoking like a cigar;
forget all that cross-Pacific longing for packed beaches,
for the roadstead where sailing ships met,
for blue jeans faded as Antarctica sky.
All they ever deliver here
are cardboard boxes full of computer parts,
as if there is nothing outside the computer,
but some boxes, I believe, contain pizza.

## DIABOLICAL UTTERANCES

Raise the devil as a hot dust storm,
to settle as warm volcanic ash.
If the devil catches you idle,
he'll turn you into a vandal.

When the devil hangs about your neck,
he'll make you a nervous wreck.
When the devil whispers, You are handsome,
your ears will go red as brimstone.

They say in every town the devil has his day,
and every devil has a town in mind.
There are only seven angels in harmony,
and nine devils of discord.

Can you handle the jandal
in the company of the devil?
Let the devil take the hindquarters,
and let the lawyers do due diligence.

Raise no more devils than you can lay down,
but never renounce the devil,
till you have a fine wardrobe.
The devil climbs the beech tree to sleep with the bats.

The devil needs martyrs and you'll do.
The devil is a subtle debater,
and can lead you by ear, nose
and throat to emergency surgery.

The devil rocks up on all fronts
to swing and swag his brag.
The devil's horns are fluorescent
and will serve to light the way.

When you call to the devil,
don't mention my name.

## GORGON

I follow the hollow
to influence the whole.
I rage-tweet my role
at what they stole.
I croon to the moon,
then churn to a burn.
I enter the centre
to dissent from my mentor.
I centennial my millennial
to keep from the fentanyl.
I boomer at the rumour
that I'm in a coma.
I clickety-clack at yackety-yak.
I lah-de-dah from afar.
I puzzle over my muzzle,
and freedom fry shoo-flies.
I precariat the commentariat.
I'm pissed I'm on the list,
and I debate my hate.
I supremacist my cyst.
I cancel them mandibles,
and no platform that unicorn.
I high-five the hive,
and vape-smoke the woke.
I discourse from my high horse,
and tap-post my boast.

I am the gorgon stare of a Predator drone.
I am a witch doctor pointing the bone.
I am the question mark of an olive branch.
I am hellfire from Paradise Ranch.

A was executed by a catapult stone.
B died as a defender of the status quo.
Trolls to the right of me; to the left are ogres.
On side with the gorgon, which side am I on?

I am listening to your bleep, sending me to sleep.
You got the dessert trolley, the cheese trolley,
the drinks trolley and the carving trolley —
they go all the way down tinfoil hat alley.

## MY PHONE

Carry success in the back pocket,
don't need a neck locket,
my phone.

Tinny incantations,
buds trailing jellyfish tentacles,
my phone.

A posture of prayer,
and a deep stare,
my phone.

More present there,
not somewhere but everywhere,
my phone.

Chosen avatar
taps out a scansion measure,
my phone.

Enthralled by the particular,
keep the screen perpendicular,
my phone.

Each waved, a gazillion wands,
on sea-jewel screen-saved,
my phone.

Skip from everlasting to everlasting
with beating wing,
my phone.

You're alone unless
you have —
my phone.

Trance walk, exodus talk;
lamentation, revelation,
my phone.

Smash phone, mash phone,
playing memory's ringtone,
my phone.

I've been hacked and my movements tracked
by a dating app on
my phone.

The payphone has a bone to pick with corrections,
and I don't have a cellphone in my cell to get directions —
my phone.

You got me caught between phone separation anxiety,
the devil and the deep blue sea —
my phone.

I left my dumb phone at home, but I no longer know
where that is: the smart phone is my comfort zone —
my phone.

All the commercials squeal and drone;
all the dragons' teeth are sown;
algorithms drill algebra down to the bone;
there's a dawn chorus of ringtones —
my phone.

## BEATRICE

Sleep fled, and I felt, in my ice-cold cheeks,
The colour fade, which it is bound to do
In any face that feels fear, or wonder,
Shock or awe, for she had burst the bubble
Of my assumptions, and taken a chainsaw to the door.

I watched her plunge into the infinity pool,
A naked singularity on my
Event horizon, the oracle of my days,
Who caught me with the black holes of her eyes,
Stole a glance, led me through the kissing gate.
We waltzed by the coin-in-slot waterfall,
We tangoed through the plastic foliage,
As white-collar managers frowned and clamoured.

She stalked my nights and took over my life,
She was my shoe-thrower, my whistleblower,
Till I raised a white flag from the wreckage.
She left me bobbing in the turbulence
Of her furious wake, of her vanguard's
Slipstream, her déjà voodoo, her time creep.

She drove her tractor through my field of dreams,
She defragged my every humble brag.
She was my homing missile, my drone pilot
Above the desert, faster than a speeding camel,
As, hands on my head, I hurried for the hills.

Her name was Beatrice, her dad owned the hotel,
I was the sky-pool's lifeguard attendant.
We became a couple: me, Gloomy Gus,

And she Goody Two-Shoes, in search of thrills.
She put me through Hell and Purgatory,
Now my memory's a bulldozed ghost town.
I move in a mall coma, these latter days.
My cheeks' colour has never bloomed again,
The angelic mandolins are long gone.

## HANG ON SOAPY

I worry about money; you worry about abusive family.
I'm the weird girl; you are too normal.
He is the adored handsome son who wants a sex change.
She's into self-harm and the beauty of privilege.
I believe in flashbacks; you live only for the future.
Your anxiety attacks precede my bereavements.
Too many bitchy friends make for a bad brew.
Your earrings are cherries on a tree in Central.
They say everyone feels a bit light-headed,
now that the mall has been spritzed with scent.
She never toppled into the tub of purple,
treading out the soapy grapes of vintage
in jealousy, the jealousy of someone who saw
creative writing students confide in each another.
The endangered frog is green with chlorophyll.
I wish I was just one of the everyday people,
for I am green too, green to the gills,
yet cushioned from worlds of hurt by you.

## TOO MANY DAVES

defibrillator dave
snaggle-toothed dave
hair-like-a-frightwig dave
dave the rave
howzat dave
first among daves
preppy Sixties TV dave
oh my sigh sigh dave
small ruby pilot light dave
the dave crew
tidal dave
let's see what dave brings
daves of wine and roses
daves of Counties Manukau
tee-hee dave
the last daves of mankind
another dead dave
it's all about dave
dave by dave
they are many

## AFTERLIFE

I would dig a bigger slice of the roseate
radiance that spins elusive in a pink cloud
beyond my fingertips, but as someone
slips and slides from the ski slope every day,
headed for the biggest boulder around,
so my immortal soul turns the corkscrew
to an afterlife of booze and cigarettes
with hammered skin and the skull knuckled.
I make promises to the rock of ages,
then break it up to pave the planet.
Your otter-skin pelt skims through the glittery
browed sea on a trip beyond me.
I drop like a sparrowhawk on a pigeon,
or spider on wasp, run like a Norway rat
up a limb to a forking dilemma and fall.
I have swum with the green sea turtle,
pondered a Victorian table,
and questioned the biblical fable,
till it reared up and flew back to bite me,
who was unvaccinated and turned rabid.
I raged like a loon against the hideous moon
that glowed like a spoon over a lamp
to bubble tar, and drew up my blood
into a quasar doused with helium;
the resultant explosion lit the stars
and kept me staring into space
just twelve steps below paradise.

## ODE FOR IGGY POP

Iggy getting jiggy rocks the mike,
Iggy in skinny jeans and fat suit top,
Iggy tied up in contortionist knots,
flicks the snaky cable, likes to prance a lot.
Iggy's resting not resting grumpy face
changes to his smiley-face lust for life.
Great survivor of the Cretaceous Age,
gonk feet, gonk hair and wobbly belly,
he's a roaring dinosaur in the sunset,
who's not quite ready to go extinct yet.
The groovy one's now grooved all over,
he's dirty old rock and roll, out to clover,
that voice sexed up with nitrous oxide,
bud smoke curling like something chronic.
Iggy Stooge, mother-naked, flexes his biceps.
With gummy mouth and excitable chin,
his face has fallen like rumpled pantyhose.
Protected specimen in witness protection,
he's a smorgasbord, a feast, torso all jelly,
tongue like a gherkin, eyes like pickled onions,
arms like pretzel sticks, pasty eyelids.
Going to see the man known as Iggy Pop,
in a world where corporates quarry rock,
guitars going for it and drummer's mighty hammer,
Iggy revs that tongue to slobber and stammer.
He's the passenger who will ride and ride.
The cavernous jowls of his face possess
shadows in which adoring fans might hide.
He's indignant in indigo and deep purple haze,
he snarls and he twitches but remains unfazed.
Iggy Pop, Iggy Pop, Iggy Pop, star still on top,

rebel without a cause, enters through the exit doors.
Even mouldy with mildew and muddy like a grave,
he thumps his chest, an Apache brave.
Dharma bum, yogi mystic, loco hobo,
down on the dance floor with wild wild voodoo.
Iggy Pop, Iggy Pop, Iggy Pop, star still on top.
He's Iggy Pop, Iggy Pop, and he ain't gonna stop.

## HOMAGE TO *FAHRENHEIT 451*

Index of what's forbidden, incunabula,
completist compendium, the great codex,
gospels, epistles, illuminated missals,
Sibyl's leaves, pith taken from trunks of trees.
Book of facts, book of feasts, book of legends,
book of nonsense, book of lies, book of dreams,
book of lost tribes, book of enlightenment,
bleeding edge of devil's ink, one more time.
Book of annihilation, defacement; book thrown,
book that bites and stings to free us from us;
book buried full fathom five, made of bone.
The Viking epic, the Hindu epic, the Dunciad,
even the novel Elizabethan world-view,
dumped on the cart, books sacred or taboo;
books forgotten: asked, what happened to you?
Books extant, bow down; now out on their ear:
each extinct volume stamped Not Made Here.
Books judged guilty till proved innocent.
Literature blown up to very fine scraps:
fragments stuck like wings of bees in amber;
books like a squarish chunk of the True Cross.
The farce of dustiny, backward and abysmal,
a negation that rejects the universal;
leaping from pages into your arms no more;
instead, remaindered and trucked for landfill.
Gore Vidal's four favourite words: I told you so;
but who is to know Oscar Wilde tore off
the corner of each page he read with the flourish
of an orchestra conductor, entombed
along with his books, as a waka sinks on Taupō.
Laws to purify the dialect of the tribe;

remember us, whisper words of wisdom,
though passports revoked, they're shipped off-shore.
Cathedral where logomancers once held sway,
the gulf of which Horace wrote and Homer sang
is as empty as a bureaucrat's head;
and those are dollar signs that were her eyes.
Light creates place, but print is meaning plain,
while absence is melancholy, an ode by John Keats.
God's anvil, smote by McCahon's paintbrush, was built
for Jerusalem with Blake's Holy Word.
Archaic zeal unhouses a legacy,
a bookish harvest crushed to root out heresy.
Dust is dust, and that vaulted ambition
of collections past, a quaint old custom.
Let some muscular aphorist rip shit or bust
this slow-grown forest for Amazon chopsticks.
It's the same mess made yesterday —
as the landscape erodes in today's rain —
when conserving was a dirty word in boardrooms.
Beware jabberwocks with their tape measures,
beware contempt of performative franchises,
beware the down-under of the spirit,
grim resistance of civil puritans.
So slash the library until it bleeds,
outsource consultation of our needs;
give books to the collector of leftover souls.
*Urne Buriall*, Urquhart's Rabelais, all are gone.
Books are noble animals but have to be put down,
because about suffering they are never wrong.
Out of the crooked timber of humanity,
no straight thing was ever made, except books:
books, now martyrs to electronic buzzfuzz,
cancel culture and bonfires of the vanities,

airy nothings of populist politicians.
You screen, I screen, we all screen together.
I dig your screen; screen on, it's a lovely feeling;
your smartphone screen has got me reeling.
Slam the book shut and get with the programme:
a mass indoctrination by the corporation.
Put books through a paper shredder;
kill the arcane tome, you'll feel better.

## An Apparition of Books

I have a hymn book in a hatbox.
I have a Bible chained to a table.
I have a book that could only have emanated
from a criminal lunatic asylum.
I have a book to bury your bonce in,
and dig it up again,
once the worms have picked it clean,
leaving a grinning skull.
I have a book larded with lunacies
and blasphemous licence —
a book on the Index Expurgatorius,
that to read is a sin against the Holy Ghost.
But a book that remains shut is just a block of wood.
I have a book with a broken spine,
lying face-down on the floor.
I have a book, dog-eared, battered,
pulpy, rained-on, buckled,
that has tumbled along the street.
I have a book with lepidoptera pressed
between the pages.
I have a book with dried poppy juice
nestled lightly in its gutter.
I have a book with chapters stuck together
by the lees of a full-bodied red wine.
I have a book made brittle by the sun,
the ink printed on its paper
barely able to be made out,
even with a magnifying glass.
My multitude of books blossoms like a tree.

## THE BOOK THROWER

She threw the book across the room.
She threw the book at him.
She defaced the book.
She tore up the book.
She burned the book.
She buried the book.
She wrote the book.

They learned the book.
They loved the book.
You fled the book.
You avoided the book.
You tripped over the book.
Your curled around the book.
You read the book.

# THE SQUILLIONAIRE

*These city areas are riddled with iceberg basements belonging to oligarchs,*
*autarks and arms merchants.*

To see an infinity pool
in the palm of your hand
and global investment
within an hour ...
A pseudo-library is being built for you,
fake book bindings await your pleasure:
they all hold expensive liquor.

Bring on luxury brands to excite me,
tote bags to bite me;
my shoes locked in fetters of silver.
I have gold-clad over-reach,
I have, of course, a private beach.
I have a master's degree
in applied authenticity,
and at the final climate summit,
I promise you full authority
to apply a compulsory purchase order.

## GOG AND MAGOG

The sun goes down; the twin peaks
of Gog and Magog stand together.
Gog's eye springs open; Magog's mouth closes.
Gog jogs on; Magog plays mahjong.
Gog's wounds rain down. Magog's foot's gone to sleep.
Gog's bod is at odds with Magog's noggin.
Gog's gone widdershins; spins into a bog.
Magog's got hooks into Gog's sooks.
Magog plays leapfrog; Gog's agog.
Magog's befogged; Gog feels odd.
Doggone, by Gogwottery; egad, by Magog's blood.
Strewth, Gog's truth runs into Magog's demagoguery.
Gog and Magog giggle and goggle all night long;
then the sun comes up over their twin peaks again.

## I Want to Write a Poem

I want to write a poem
        the colour of paracetamol,
        the colour of pinot noir.
I want to write a poem
        like an impetuous kiss;
        a poem like a sloth,
        reaching for the last jungle branch
        before the plantation begins.
I want to write a poem
        like a tight-rope walker
        between the Twin Towers,
        lit up by rays of another sun
        and a heavenly host of planets,
        announcing God is great.
I want to write a poem
        like a box kite,
        a poem like a blue-sky day,
        a poem like a nor'wester in summer.
I want to write a poem
        like a rusted car wreck,
        like a collapsed bridge,
        like a random punch,
        like a sly foot-tap,
        like a Māori haka,
        like a fresh death mask,
        like peel-off future proofing,
        like the smile of a stolen girlfriend,
        like the scent of Adieu Sagesse,
        like gravestones, like time-bombs,
        fractal geometry, orchestra tom-toms.

I want to write a poem
>> like the twilight zone,
>> like righteous incarceration,
>> like the steady pit-pat of the rain.

## DEEPWATER HORIZON

The fountainhead splutters,
the drilling falters.
Drill, baby, drill;
never mind the spill;
but the top kill tanked;
the whole Gulf huffs the fumes.
Pelicans and dolphins read the runes
written in oil slick
on sacred texts of saltwater,
and then choke.
The ocean's white lace
blackens in blotched eclipse;
waves anoint beaches with gunk,
their cup runneth over.
Starfish go belly up,
beneath oozing sludge.
How much oil can an oyster-shucker shuck?
The oil tycoon up on his stilt platform
is a matador who drapes a dark cape,
fanning a trillion smears.
Greased by raw crude, shining bright,
the face of capitalism hides her scars.
A CEO in a burlap sack
circus-dives towards a barrel of bitumen
from a great height.
Those are oil bubbles that were his words.
In choppers
another Chief;
sad laughter of wind-up clacking teeth
announces
business as usual.

## THE RIGHT HONOURABLE ORDER OF AUSTRALIAN PRIME MINISTERS

Cool kookaburra laughter, auguries of marsupial heartbeats,
prime minister after prime minister carried off by dingoes.
Reading tracks of flightless birds, lied to by the lyrebird,
August as Menzies, serene as Hawke, anchored by a schooner.
Nah, not a chance, when Abbott sees God in his Speedos deny Uluru three times.
He shirt-fronts, like a boxing kangaroo. Our chapel perilous is crowded;
will no one rid us of this troublesome priest? Secret whitefella business,
speared by ancient Murdoch, and scorched on a barbecue to incineration.
Growled flights of blasphemy sail towards snags and beer.
He arrived with the wattle flower. He arrived as a barbarous barber.
His Grand Guignol shaves clean as a guillotine.
The cherubic cheeks of the press pack blow along the clouds.
How goes it? How grows it? The last prime minister knows it.
He arrived as he intended to leave, with high fives;
but he leaves in a murdering minute, trussed up for the roast.
The locals were making hay, sauntering like lords and ladies gay,
and milking a cash cow that had wandered in, wearing a guru's garland.
Epoch lies down with epoch till doomsday;
but no one is looking for a handout,
because we're all liberals here, here for the beer.

## The End of History

1989, when the fall of Berlin's wall
chiselled away loose masonry,
brought promise for humanity,
as Tank Man stood tall in Tiananmen Square.
Dignity seemed worth more
at the end of the Cold War than ever before.
Lovers kissed for cameras, which made
every photograph special, like a bouquet,
while wires that held the whole shebang
upright were hidden well away.
They placed white carnations in rifle muzzles.
They dumped Kalashnikovs for bumpers of champagne.
They waved banners and the snare drum beat.
They climbed to the top of decline and fall.
The fix was in, nothing for it but to swim.
1989, when the world wide web's pipedream lit up;
telexes hiccupped, telephones tittered, faxes coughed,
though so many were soon to return
in coffins from whatever war was next.
Some had paintstripper to remove the pain;
some smooshed their wonted ancient grain.
Sir Galahad rode in with leather apron on,
making light of the massacre, the heavy weather,
the forked lightning, the stacks of stooks
in summer stubble, scorched for yonks.
Choppers prepared for evacuation.
Citizens rejoiced in satellites, holding hands,
blindly high on their own resolution,
across the ocean and down in the deeps,
whose dungeons opened and released the Fates,
in bubbles of oxygen that seemed herculean.

Yesterday's progress ended and was rebooted.
Deplorables became renewable; edibles became incredible.
Assemblies clanked through flung-open gates.
And you will know us by our toppled hopes;
flogged scars and stripes that bless the bloody flag.
We were going forward, the damned, on our five-year plan,
in language of prayer to stardust of paradise,
with lassoed monuments and new statues raised;
but hope is the thing that scatters,
through tarred and feathered streets,
as tear-gas arrives and water cannon swings.
There were human pyramids and plagues
of new missiles; jogging shoes hung from gallows.
The blow-up globe was punctured and hissed
with escaping breath as another dream
began to count down to lift-off;
and then we were stuck in the 1990s,
with a long night coming on,
and very few left to sing revolution's song.

## WHAT THE FUTURE HOLDS

Hear the voice of the bard who past, present and future sees,
intoned our own William Blake, James K Baxter,
in his back-to-front overcoat,
hitchhiking towards Hiruhārama,
and waiting for the future to catch up with him.
Poetry touches the soul from the beginnings of the world,
where we were once whole,
and maybe, too, reaches for Shakespearean oblivion,
where our future's in the stars.
In Māori thought, the past, the deeds of the ancestors,
is actively confronted by the living. The past is called ngā rā o mua,
the days in front. Time collapses into the continuous present,
into the long clock of now.
Our clock, though, might have been painted by Salvador Dalí.
It seems to be melting … along with the glaciers …
So, what does the future hold?
What does the future hold,
besides another flickering episode
of *Burnt Planet* narrated by the computer-generated voice
of Sir David Attenborough?
The future is no longer what it was, because we wanted flying cars —
and what we got was Twitter —
or 140 characters in a novel by Ellie Catton.
In the era of Covid-19, we locked down
to save the pāua and the glory of the nation, for the future.
It ain't nothing, so give it a name — the future.
In quantum mechanics,
the answers surround us, but we don't know the question —
call it the future.
We here in Aotearoa, with our Communist Princess leader,
are the blacksmiths of the red future,

we hammer out the keys to happiness,
living in Te Waipounamu.
The world's gone indoors, but we're rewilding parks and lawns,
and knitting together wild and woolly yarns,
for the foreseeable, for the future —
where climate change is the loose change
of conversation dropped on the food chain of the homeless,
and hedge funds light up with neoliberal domination,
and Uncle Hohum is there in the easy chair,
with all the great and the good with shiny faces,
greasy with butter and China-bound milk powder,
their casino table aces flung on a green hectare.
The future is not what it was — and may Jeff Bezos
save the Amazon, but not in his image,
and may Elon Musk turn into a skull-trinket
wreathed in the musk of *Cannabis sativa*,
and may the screw-loose, the hyper-loopies,
those who dwell in the Last Chance Saloon,
learn their fate at last …
Drought, famine, mudslide, refugee camp, bread queue —
just press that button, bro, and up we all go —
the car bleats in response to a thumbed key fob.
So spritz some Bezos into your existence,
the abracadabra of alibaba is amaze-on!
Ocean to ocean, one clearing station, amaze-on!
Container by container, metal as anything, amaze-on!
The hyper-normals are in denial about the source of the Nile,
and wearing cut-off denims and a faded tan,
and each one is a very big fan of the last one.
And there goes Elon Musk's sky-train
silver as Santa's sleigh lit by the sun's last ray
in a dark sky on Christmas Day
chugging across the Milky Way

bringing strings of satellites to every quadrant,
flagrant, vagrant, space junk in every quadrant
that's up there, binding the globe to its transponders
in perfect wonder and interstellar cold,
as we look on from our kauri tree platform,
while feral things snuffle and hoot into the early morn.

In the future, the plant managers are planet managers,
a thousand-hour day is normal,
but it only lasts a nanosecond in the long clock of now.
A psychic numbing may be your best defence.
You're tracked, parsed, mined and modified to make sense,
then caressed to find what you like best.
The right to be forgotten has been removed in jest,
but exclusion is not an option.
See the eggplant emoji that ate Chicago,
for Ford is in his flivver and we got your cargo,
and for what you want, how far will you go?
It's all gone to the great aggregator at the worm farm,
but how are you going to pay for what you just took?
It's the wisdom of Uncle Google and his little red book
down in the deep of deeps where he keeps his rest.

So what does the future hold
when they're paying attention
in the attention economy?
All those eyeballs rolling loose,
now jammed in a jam jar,
strobed by white light, white noise.
The X things only a Y would understand,
the 13 struggles all left-handers know to be true,
the 21 things the algorithm knows about you,
on this Earth, this one weeping eyeball,

where neophiliacs check their messages
looking for a weapons upgrade,
and glut upon glut has gone splut,
and the nut section of the supermarket
is the largest — anti-vaxxer nuts, conspiracy nuts, gun nuts,
science-denying nuts, religious nuts.

Nobody move. Everybody down.
Everybody reach high.
Who knows who anymore, it's always the other guy.
Get your core meaning scrambled in a blender,
then sliced and diced and sold off,
before being returned to sender.
Go ahead, encrypt the panopticon to baseline anon,
where everything is coloured high-key
and seems to offer serendipity,
as you prepare to deactivate the soc med binary.
Either stolen or broken or burning,
faster, faster, faster, yada, yadda, yadda …

But really what the future holds for you and me
is just another cup of tea,
comfort slippers and a lumpy sofa,
and quietly waiting till this Covid is over.
The future repeats as you creak up the stairs,
horrendous youth, querulous dear dears,
dry leaves falling from deciduous trees,
and no let-up on your diagnosed disease.
There's no let-up, no one stops,
all is forward momentum unto the next generation,
— and more moral panic, more fornicating in the streets,
angst in the pants and fancy-schmancy OE.
They got booths for the aged, booths for the terminal,

and a plan for a hospital that looks unwell.
But build me up, buttercup, don't break my heart,
— shouldn't the future be a brand-new start?
Dream on buster because the future's lost its lustre.
From the salt and pepper moptop of Sergeant Pepper
to the shiny busby of the American Princess Markle,
that's bolder, better, and has more sparkle,
the puppet strings of algorithms
animate us endlessly, through every kind of insecurity.
Yesterday was so five minutes ago,
it's got up and gone to Goneville again,
so everyone get on the particle accelerator,
everyone get with the giggle generator, everyone say, See you later.
Everything's correctable if it's detectable.
Eyes brighter than the eye of Sauron,
they are talking to Baby Yoda about the future.
Loud as the buzz of all the bees in bumbledom,
there's a march for equal rights by a million possums,
and, off and on, QAnon shuffle off to Buffalo.
As my autograph is my witness,
they strip-mined my data to make it their business.
How sharp is your semi-conductor?
How green is your silicon valley?
Collective murmuration, crack of starter's pistol,
draw a red rectangle around it and call it the AI recognition state,
out on the bleeding edge where the future is being made
with a twenty percent error rate.
Never too smart to learn, never too old to dance,
In End Times, the future is toast and I'm history,
escaping with a hiss, and maybe a sense of mystery.
Kia ora!

# Notes and Acknowledgements

Poems in this collection have previously appeared in: *A Cluster of Lights – Then and Now: 52 writers around the world*; *A Kind of Shelter Whakaruru-taha*; *Best Small Fictions 2021*; *Blackmail Press*; *Blueskin News*; *Broadsheet*; *Canto Planetario*; *Jacket2*; *Landfall*; *Leaps and Bounds* (Earl of Seacliff Art Workshop poetry mini-book series no. 49); *North & South*; New Zealand Poet Laureate Blog; *No Other Place to Stand: An anthology of climate change poetry from Aotearoa New Zealand*; *New Zealand Herald*; NZ Poetry Shelf; *Okay, Boomer*; *Otago Daily Times*; *Otakou Press*; *Percutio*; *Poetry New Zealand*; Phantom Billstickers Poems on Posters; *Roar, Squeak, Purr: A New Zealand treasury of animal poems*; *Sweet Mammalian*; *Takahē*; *The Anthology of Love for the Book*; *The Aotearoa New Zealand Performance Poetry Anthology*; *Throw Net | Upena Hoʻolei* (Fernbank Studio chapbook series); *Turbine*; *The Spinoff*; *VERB Journal*; and *World Poetry Tree*.

'fridge magnet poem' was composed from a standard magnetic sheet of word tiles. 'What the Future Holds' was first delivered at the Dunedin Writers & Readers Festival 2021 Gala Showcase, 'What Does the Future Hold?'. 'Te Wheke' was originally commissioned for WHEKE!, an event planned as part of the Aotearoa New Zealand Festival of the Arts 2022.

'Hone' was composed at the invitation of publisher Donald Kerr, in conjunction with the Otakou Press and the Centre for the Book at the University of Otago, together with the UNESCO City of Literature office in Dunedin, and the Hone Tuwhare Trust, for a hand-printed publication celebrating the centenary of poet Hone Tuwhare's birth.

Most of these poems were written while I held the New Zealand Poet Laureate Award (August 2019 to August 2022), which is administered by the National Library of New Zealand Te Puna Mātauranga o Aotearoa. I would like to thank laureate kaitiaki Peter Ireland, chief librarian Chris Szekely and national librarian Rachel Esson for their support.

I wish to acknowledge the support of Fulbright-Creative New Zealand Pacific Writer's Residency and my time at the University of Hawaiʻi at Mānoa Campus in Honolulu for two and a half months at the end of 2018, which provided inspiration and insight for the section titled 'The Death of Kapene Kuke', completed in 2021.

I am also grateful for fourteen days at the Michael King Writers Centre in Devonport, Auckland, in February 2020, which allowed me space, time and perspective to write a number of poems based around Tāmaki Makaurau.

I would like to thank my brother Tonu Shane for the concept of and motivation for the 'Whale Song' section, intended to celebrate the mana of the whale.

I am grateful to Steve Reekie for permission to use his 2022 photograph of the rusted wheels of an old coal truck, located in a Te Waipounamu West Coast rainforest, on the cover of *Respirator*.

Special thanks to Anna Hodge for her editorial acumen and to the team at Otago University Press for their sterling production work on *Respirator*.

Fạiåkse`ea, malo `aupito and gratitude to my whānau nui for all the ongoing support.

*Respirator* is dedicated to the memory of my mother and father for their guiding influence and encouragement, always.

Published by Otago University Press
Te Whare Tā o Te Wānanga o Ōtākou
533 Castle Street
Dunedin, New Zealand
university.press@otago.ac.nz
www.otago.ac.nz / press

First published 2023
Copyright © David Eggleton
The moral rights of the author have been asserted.

ISBN 978-1-99-004850-0

Published with the assistance of Creative New Zealand and
the National Library of New Zealand Te Puna Mātauranga o Aotearoa

ARTS COUNCIL OF NEW ZEALAND *TOI AOTEAROA*

Editor: Anna Hodge
Cover photograph: Steve Reekie, Coal truck wheels, West Coast, 2022

Printed in China through Asia Pacific Offset